# Table of Contents

# Primer

# VIII. The Incumbency Blues

# IX. A Challenger Rises From the Mean Streets of Bloomfield Hills

# x. The Most Important Election in the History of America. Again.

# Foreword

**Q.** For whom is this book intended?

**A.** This book is designed as a comprehensive guide to the 2012 Presidential Election for potential voters and non-voters alike.

**Q.** What do you mean by potential non-voters?

**A.** People who haven't read the book.

**Q.** Any particular sort of potential voter?

**A.** Potential voters of all types: the decided, the undecided, the almost, kind of, really close to, near-the-vicinity-of decided and the you-couldn't-budge-me-with-anything-less-than-a-$300,000-direct-deposit-into-my-Swiss Bank Account decided.

**Q.** What questions does this book answer?

**A.** Easy questions. Hard questions. Any question that could possibly be answered by a series of smartass, cynical, semi-schmaltzy, highly acerbic, humorist-type ramblings. Even stupid questions. Remember there are no stupid question only Low Information Voters.

**Q.** What does that mean?

**A.** Low Information Voter is a new demographic category that means "stupid people." But the great thing is—you get to say it right in front of them. ROTFLMFAOLARTB.

**Q.** Got an example?

**A.** A recent poll shows 52% of Mississippi Republicans still believe President Obama is Muslim. And that doesn't include the hefty percentage who believe he's muslin.

**Q.** Isn't that a loosely woven cotton fabric?

**A.** Correctamundo. And yes, it does tend to confuse them, but it's a state to which they've become accustomed.

**Q.** You mean Mississippi.

**A.** Exactly. Now you've got it.

**Q.** Got what?

**A.** I don't know, but it's all over the front of your shirt. Go directly to the bathroom and wash it off. Immediately after purchasing the book, that is.

Become a Hyperink reader. Get a special surprise.

Like the book? Support our author and leave a comment!

# Tale O' the Tape

|  | Willard Mitt Romney | Barack Hussein Obama |
|---|---|---|
| **Alias.** | Mormon Money Man. | Black Moses. |
| **Age.** | 65 | 51 |
| **College.** | Stanford/ Brigham Young/ Harvard Business | Occidental / Colombia/ Harvard Law |
| **Height.** | 6' 0" | 6' 1" |
| **Weight.** | 185 | 176 |
| **Zodiac.** | Pisces | Leo |
| **Chinese Zodiac.** | Year of the Pig. | Year of the Ox. |
| **Reach.** | Right down Wall Street. | Edge of Main Street. |
| **Nickname.** | Mittens | Barry |
| **Birthplace.** | Detroit, Michigan | Honolulu, Hawaii |
| **Stance.** | Center Right | Center Left |
| **Record.** | 1 win, 1 loss | 5 wins, 1 loss |
| **Titles.** | King of Bain. | Prince of Peace. |
| **Go To Phrase.** | Failure of Leadership. | Could Have Been Worse. |
| **Potential turnovers.** | Lack of human emotion. | Lack of party support. |

| | | |
|---|---|---|
| **Strengths.** | Hair. Teeth. Checkbook. | Incumbency. |
| **Weaknesses.** | RomneyCare. | ObamaCare. |
| **Assists.** | Salt Lake City Olympics. | Joe Biden. |
| **Dog.** | Seamus. | Bo. |
| **Blocks.** | Gingrich & Santorum. | Clinton Crime Family. |
| **Steals.** | Florida & Michigan. | Moral High Ground. |
| **Jab.** | Money. | Rationality. |
| **Hook.** | Money. | Impartiality. |
| **Uppercut.** | Money. | Diplomacy. |
| **Killer instinct.** | Questionable. | Highly Suspect. |
| **Quality of opponents.** | Highly Suspect. | Questionable. |
| **Athleticism.** | Goes well to right. | Loves middle of ring. |
| **Footwork.** | Can't dance. | Dances well. |
| **Endurance.** | Untested. | Unestablished. |
| **Strategic skills.** | Linear. | Evolved. |
| **Corner.** | Gilded. | Focused. |
| **Defense mechanism.** | Pummel them with money. | Talk them into submission. |
| **Don't bring that up.** | London Olympics. | The economy. |
| **Or that.** | # of Cadillacs wife owns. | Unemployment. |

# III.

# Handicapping the Race

# Or... a vague approximation of how we got here.

On November 4, 2008, Barack Hussein Obama was elected 44th President of the United States. And liberals and progressives all over the country rejoiced. Political comedians: not so much. Bush was a satirical mother lode. Like if Reagan and Quayle had a kid. A Wheel of Fortune President in a Jeopardy world. Even Clinton hit the ground running as a corpulent womanizer. But Obama was smoother than chamois on chrome, affording little if any purchase to hook satirical barbs onto. Besides, you can't mock Hope. Too much like kicking a small furry whimpering thing with big eyes. Had to wait for Hope to scab over a bit. Didn't have to wait long. In this chapter we'll chronicle just a few of the chafing dishes served up under the sneeze guard at the hot topics buffet.

# 5 Presidents

*Hailing a landmark occasion with a few hallmark observations.*

*(Photo Courtesy of Jeannene Hansen)*

It is the wackiest photo-op since Sarah Palin went herself a-turkey-farming. 3 ex presidents, the current president and the future president all kicking it old school, chilling in the Oval Office talking about what cool carpeting abounds. The five of them together IS a great image. And if Barack Obama remains serious about that economic stimulus plan of his, we could raise a ton of money selling poster-sized copies of this historic gathering for use as a bipartisan dartboard. And George the Younger conveniently positioned himself dead center middle to act as an organic bulls eye.

What the New York Post dubbed Club Prez was either a power lunch on steroids or the world's most exclusive fraternity hazing. Can't you just imagine the elders pranking Obama with a dribble glass or faking news of a Pakistani nuke strike on Kashmir? Nobody knows what subjects were breached, but the general consensus is personal experience was offered up as advice. For instance, the Bush boys and Jimmy Carter might have cautioned against getting stuck in the quicksand of the Middle East and Bill Clinton probably advocated the installation of an in-house dry cleaning operation. I'd love to report the five of them fought like perturbed raccoons, knocking over furniture and bloodily emerging with torn lapels and black eyes, but no, they all sucked it up and played nice. I'm sure nobody wanted to answer to Laura if anything happened to the new china.

The Oval Office bonding photo is destined to become as iconic as that Vegas snapshot of the Rat Pack outside the Sands that people regularly Photoshop themselves into. Although, the only insertable gap in the photo appears between Clinton and Carter, who reportedly get along like tinfoil and teeth. Something having to do with who deserved the title of "Mister Peace Maker" back in the 90s and who deserved "Mr. Grandstander." Jimmy Carter (and isn't he getting a bit long in the tooth to be called Jimmy?) is starting to exude that smug self-righteousness you normally associate with your priggish Aunt Hoogolah. Starting to look like her too.

As lease-holder of the residence where lunch was held, Dubyah was the very soul of genial host, but does appear to be chomping at the bit to get the hell out of public housing. "I want to thank the President-Elect for joining the Ex-Presidents for lunch" forgetting he's contractually obligated to stick around until January 20th. Complaints arose that Obama upstaged the President by addressing the press. But come on, upstaging George Bush? At this point, a #2 pencil stuck in a ceiling tile could upstage Bush the Younger.

This is only the second time in recent memory anybody's seen such a congregation of POTUSes and I doubt the fancy-word guys have come up with a plural moniker yet. So here's our chance for linguistic immortality. There's the old favorites. Assembly. Army. Pride. Quiver. Swarm. Parliament. Clutch. Caucus. Mob. But while Parliament of POTUSes is intriguing, I'm shooting for something more suitable—like what they use for locusts: "a plague." Or maybe the lapwings: a deceit. Stud of mares—yeah, you wish. Closer to a prickle of porcupines. Labor of moles. An unkindness of ravens. Shiver of sharks. Lamentation of swans. Mutation of thrushes. Nah, none of those really work. Gaggle? Giggle? Google? Sludge, snort, flutter, bloat? Jamboree? No. No. No. Wait. I got it. A Port-a-Potty of POTUSes. Inimitable, alliterative and apt.

**Highly Instructive ELECT TO LAUGH! Quote:** "The best argument against democracy is a five-minute conversation with the average voter." Winston Churchill.

# Democracy Is the New Black

*Welcoming the revolting flocks of the Mid East with a few cautionary notes about freedom.*

Congratulations from the United States of America to all our freedom loving brothers and sisters in Egypt and Yemen and Jordan and Oman and Tunisia and Libya and Iran and Bahrain and Morocco and Algeria and maybe someday soon Saudi Arabia for standing up to your dictatorial overlords and clutching at the guano covered branches of freedom. Jolly good. You've made majority rule fashionable again. Democracy is the new black.

We are all totally psyched how you've dragged yourselves kicking and screaming from the dark ages into the middle 19th Century. You may be excited to hear about some other upgrades we've made in areas such as in transportation, communications, and hygiene. It's all there in your orientation packet. Watch some MTV. Ignore Jersey Shore. No, they're not real.

Got to warn you though, self-rule isn't all a bed of roses. It has a thorny learning curve. Rubs rough on beginners. You might want to spend some time wading out towards the deep end wearing your feudal water wings before jumping straight into the parliamentary pool.

Thing is, don't expect the world to change overnight. England has been dancing with democratization since the thirteenth century and they're still curtseying to the Queen. Usually what happens is you lose one tyrannical despot only to gain another. You could avoid a particular mistake we made and find someone who can spell despot.

Elections are tricky things. Make sure it's The People deciding the outcome and not nine old folks wearing black robes. Here's a hint: if anybody ever gets over 75% of the vote, reboot. You might be surprised to find the people most likely to run for political office turn out to be criminally insane. Maybe you should pass a law restricting that. Kind of wish we had. Rule of thumb: anybody who can be elected, shouldn't be.

Something else to keep in mind: democracy for one, means democracy for all. It's a take it or leave it enterprise. All men are created equal. And women. None of this wife-walking-five-paces-behind-her-husband-dressed-as-a-grieving-beekeeper stuff. Same with Sunnis and Shiites and Sasquatches. One person. One vote. Hey, we all put on our robes one leg at a time. Or two. Whatever.

Start small. Too many choices can result in inaction. An example: sometimes you just want a package of sunflower seeds. Original flavor. But Safeway is all out of Original because they allotted equal shelf space to the Low Sodium Dill Pickle flavor. Which nobody wants. It's there, if they wanted. But they don't. Well, same deal with liberty. So, there you are. Hope that clears that up.

All we're trying to say is good luck with the whole democracy thing. Treat it like a new car, always driving as if 100 eggs are hatching inside of it at all times. Because they are. Bring it in for a tune-up every 10,000 miles and don't forget to change the oil. (shouldn't be a problem) Remember to always downshift headed uphill; it tends to veer to the left on straightaways and try not to total the puppy because who knows, we here in America might want to give it another test drive ourselves someday.

**Highly Instructive ELECT TO LAUGH! Quote:** "If voting changed anything, they'd make it illegal." Emma Goldman

# Super Duper Congress

*Investigating the committee with special powers that promises to be a thorn in Congress's side. Or is it the Justice League?*

Oh sure, they made a big show of signing the debt ceiling agreement, with official photo-ops and fancy commemorative pens all accompanied by great racking sighs of relief. But now both Congress and the President are having second thoughts; treating the deal like a dead horsefly floating in their cut-glass tumbler of 25 year-old single malt Scotch. You'd find more enthusiasm from the contestants of a beach volleyball tournament surveying a sand court littered with scorpions scurrying under a sea of broken beer bottles.

Speaking of insects, included in the agreement was a provision forming a committee responsible for future deficit reduction. 12 members appointed by party leaders from both the House and Senate. Whose mission, should they accept it, is to find 1.5 trillion dollars over a ten year period digging deep past the bare bones, down to the marrow.

Charged to construct a plan by Thanksgiving Eve or risk triggering automatic cuts. Doomsday cuts. Cuts designed to frighten politicians from the most stable of districts. That's right: defense cuts.

A majority of the committee, equally split between Republicans and Democrats, must agree on the proposal to send it to the whole of Congress who will vote either up or down with no amendments or filibusters allowed: meaning one member has to cross party lines, which is about as likely as pimento flavored Velveeta taking first place in the 2012 World Championship Artisan Cheese Contest.

Even though the American public and pretty much every economist on the face of the planet agrees we need a balance between entitlement cuts and revenue enhancement, the Democrats have already angrily snapped that entitlement cuts are off the table and the Republicans are rigidly repeating no new revenue will be accepted, so really, what they did was not so much kick the can down the road, but throw it onto the back of a passing flatbed truck where it quickly disappeared over an asphalt horizon.

Now, this group has been called many things. Useless. Business as Usual. The

Supercommittee. Twerpy Twelve. A Dozen Punters. The Craven Caucus. Esteemed Assembly of the Ill-Advisable. League of the Unexceptionally Pontificating Pool of Party Hacks. But most interestingly, is referred to as: "Super Congress."

"Slower than a slug on Thorazine; less powerful than a soggy Kleenex; unable to compromise in a million years. Look! Up in that swiveling leather club seat of that private jet. It's a ruse, it's a sham, it's... Super Congress.

"Yes, Super Congress. Strange hybrid from another reality, come to Capitol Hill with powers and abilities far beyond those of mortal members.

"Super Congress. Who can change the course of appropriations, bend ethics regulations in the wink of an eye and who, disguised as... the United States Congress Joint Select Committee on Deficit Reduction, mild mannered functionary of the Hall of Invertebrates, fights the never ending battle against Truth, Justice, and the American Way."

And when their capes are discarded and utility belts back in storage, we can move onto the next level of logical suspension and form the Super Duper Congress. Then... Son of Super Duper Congress. And call in Batman or maybe the Justice League or reconvene the Watchmen or that little guy who talks backwards and doesn't make any sense. Mr. Mxyztplk. You may know him as: Mitch McConnell. More scorpions, please.

**Highly Instructive ELECT TO LAUGH! Quote:** "In democracy the poor will have more power than the rich, because there are more of them and the will of the majority is supreme." Aristotle.

# Trickle Up Economics

*Report from the front lines of the class war from the perspective of a draftee.*

It's all just a dance, really. A Democratic president summons the courage to call for higher taxes on the rich and Republicans cry like third graders having their ice cream taken away and given to the neighbor's dog. Invoking the hoariest of chestnuts; that oldie but goodie; as predictable as mushy green grapes in a fruit salad: The Class War Boogie.

When taxes are raised on the rich, that's class warfare, but when subsidies are handed out to giant corporations who siphon jobs offshore so that rich people can have more money, that's Trickle-Down Economics. What Barack should do is rename his efforts to balance the playing field, "Trickle-Up Economics." That would at least confuse them. Although after watching the last couple of debates, confusion seems not to be in too short of supply.

We're not even allowed to call them rich anymore. They're "job creators" now. And yes, jobs are being created. In Singapore. And Vietnam. And China. Of course at 4 bucks a gallon, that commute is going to be a bitch.

The American Dream is alive and well, just not here. It's our own damn fault, really. American workers have ruined everything with their irrational demands for safe working conditions and a living wage. Who do we think we are? Stockholders?

Republicans have been more strident than a looped siren in a stainless steel silo in their opposition to a specific Obama proposal called the Buffett Rule, which calls for billionaires like Warren Buffett to pay the same tax rate as their secretaries. The GOP prefers the Jimmy Buffett Rule, which holds that anybody worried about rent should start drinking Margaritas until they pass out.

You know what, they're right. It is a class war. The rich started it and their side is winning. Most of us didn't enlist. We were drafted. 40% of all income gains in the last decade have trickled up to the wealthiest 1%. The richest 400 families in this country control more money than the bottom 155 million people put together. We're moving from Depression levels of income inequality into French Revolution territory. Hey, isn't that Madame LaFarge over there, knitting some guillotine hoods? Naw, just somebody handing out free

Netflix subscriptions.

What is it with the rich? How much money do they need? How many Bentleys can one person drive? How many beluga caviar cream cheese canapés can be consumed at a single cocktail party? Onto how many silk pajamas with platinum threads can you spill your Dom Perignon White Gold Mimosa at a time? Okay, three. That's what the maid is for. Well, one of the things.

And these are the people complaining about a class war? You want rules, how bout the Rolex Tourbillon Rule? Mandating that anybody wearing a watch worth more than a house in Sheboygan who ever mentions class war, gets a hose shoved down their throat and goose liver pumped in until they leak pate from the ears. Less war-like, more food-fightyish. Let them eat pate.

**Highly Instructive ELECT TO LAUGH! Quote:** "Being in politics is like being a football coach. You have to be smart enough to understand the game and dumb enough to think it's important." Eugene McCarthy.

# Find the Brightside. The BP Oil Spill Edition

- All shrimp dishes guaranteed to be pre-marinated.

- Frolicsome beachside tar ball fights.

- Squeaky oysters a thing of the past.

- Gulf Coast salad dressing: just add vinegar.

- Lubricated Jelly Fish.

- Mortared with oil and tar, sand castles now tide-proof.

- Far fewer silly election year cries of "Drill, Baby, Drill."

- Need an oil change? Wander down to water's edge and squeegee a pelican.

- No more drilling for oil. Just let the oil wash right up to you.

- Romantic beach bonfires 24/7.

- Wriggling out of that tight bathing suit now a breeze.

- Every Gulf dock and pier instantly doubles as a Slip and Slide.

- Jet Skis able to refuel mid-trip.

**Highly Instructive ELECT TO LAUGH! Quote:** "I can make them voting machines sing Home Sweet Home." Huey Long.

# The Delta of Denial

*A capsule travelogue of our nation's capital.*

Slamming DC. It may be the singular most popular political game played today. Everybody's doing it. Even incumbents go out of their way to blame Washington for whatever's wrong with the country. Like a baseball manager complaining his team suffers from a crippling lack of quality motivation.

You've heard all the buzz phrases: "Washington is not the answer, it is the problem." "The devil made both Washington and hell, and chooses to live in hell." "Washington is a cesspool." Perhaps, but why then, do they, once elected, treat it like a hot tub?

Hard to tell what disturbs critics most: the culture, the people, or the rush hour traffic on the Beltway. Don't hate the player, hate the game. The residents of our nation's capital are absolutely normal. Okay, absolutely semi-normal. Or as normal as can be, considering the 202 area code is hive mind to the largest egos in the world. At least now we know what happens when the inmates take over the asylum. And the most venally ambitious of the criminally insane manage to scramble to the top.

Nobody could ever mistake DC for the real world. It's an encapsulated bubble. A yuppie terrarium. The Florence of Malfeasance. Meta Wonk Central. A work-free drug zone. The largest Superfund site in America. Where double-sided red tape originated, and they throw it around like it's going out of style.

Don't forget though, Washington is unique. The capitals of other nations are also media and entertainment centers. The only reason to venture into DC is politics. It's a company town solely designed to support the federal government. A whale of a city, with schools of subsidiary pilot fish feeding alongside. And the lobbyists and campaign managers, barnacles sticking to the side, regularly messing with the air intake valves.

It is also happens to be the single worst place on the planet to have a conversation, because all anyone wants to talk about is themselves. And don't ask for directions. Nobody has a clue about anything, yet fervently believe they possess every answer. And some folks will go miles out of their way to confuse you, just to keep their muscles toned.

JFK said DC combined all the hospitality of the north with the efficiency of the south. Not to mention the scruples of a turkey vulture overlooking a yard full of wounded bunnies. It's a town where you always have to worry that your best friend is wearing a wire. Where "cynical" is raised to an art form. Imagine the Kardashians as elderly white guys with triple the sense of entitlement.

Washington is the Delta of Denial. Routinely demonstrated by politicians who never understand why the rest of the country holds them in such low esteem. Even though they spend millions of dollars every election cycle on ads to convince us what despicable crooks their opponents are. Not realizing the only time we trust them is when they tell us the other guy is lying. And even then, we have our doubts.

Like Hotel California, once you check in, you can never leave. After spending a couple of years in DC, as a human being, you're ruined, and can never go back to living with normal people. But hey, a person has to sleep somewhere, right? Even lobbyists. They can't go home again because the rocks under which they formerly lived are gone. Besides, the Smithsonian is nice.

**Highly Instructive ELECT TO LAUGH! Note:** In 1844, Freeman Clark, an Indiana farmer, was seriously ill on Election Day. His son carried him to the county seat to vote for state senate candidate David Kelso. Clark died on the way home. David Kelso was elected by one vote. In 1844, back when state senates elected U.S. senators, the Indiana state senate elected Edward Hannigan for U.S. senate by one vote including a vote by David Kelso. In 1845, the U.S. Senate annexed Texas by a vote of 27-25. One vote cast by Senator Hannigan from Indiana. If not for Freeman Clark's sense of civic duty, Texas might not be a state today. Son of a bitch.

Become a Hyperink reader. Get a special surprise.

Like the book? Support our author and leave a comment!

# IV.

# The GOP and Other Implausible Phenomena

# Or... the not so loyal opposition and friends.

POTUS 44 didn't quite get what you would call your major assistance from the other side of the aisle. Privately, Senate Majority Leader Mitch McConnell said, "the single most important thing we can achieve is for Barack Obama to be a one term president." Of course the public stance was, "We want to work with the President." Unh-hunh. The same way a coyote wants to utilize a nest of baby ducks. And then the Teabaggers appeared out of nowhere. And I know. I know. We're not supposed to call them Teabaggers. But *they* did for the first four months. Until someone hipped them to the fact their nickname was a euphemism for gargling testicles. But that's what happens when your movement is made up solely of angry old white guys. None of whom knows how to get on the interwebs to vet their own name. Teabaggers, for crum's sake. What came in second? Cornholers for Democracy? Did Freedom's Felchers make the short list? The One-Eyed Snakes of Liberty. Cramming it down the Communist canal. Here's a few other stellar snippets of bipartisanship we were treated to during Obama's first term.

# Tax Cut Zombies from the Planet NO!

*Recoiling from the primeval horror posed by Mitch McConnell's Walking Dead.*

The stuff of nightmares. To hear the shabby shuffle of their soft somnambulant stutter is to make your skin crawl. To see their haunted hollow eyes on the cable news shows taking no notice of their surroundings is a spiral straight into terror. The worst part is the cries of the children as they cower behind couches, hands over their ears blocking out the monotonous intonations of the mind numbing mantra-"Tax Cuts. Tax Cuts. Tax Cuts." They are the Tax Cut Zombies from the Planet No! and they are not of this earth. Okay, maybe they are, but they certainly don't live in the real world.

Citizens of America, stay in your homes. The Minority leadership has unleashed their legions of virtual undead to battle the White House's economic stimulus package with a soul sapping single-mindedness and they're still out there. "Tax cuts—good. Spending—bad." The slogan echoes mournfully off the marble halls as empty husks of conservative humanity stumble through Congress with heavy plodding steps and outstretched arms lurching from cable news microphone to cable news microphone.

It is a purely defensive tactic borne of panicky desperation as the GOP recoils from the horror of their first Congressional-Executive confrontation in 14 years lacking relevance. In the House, they stood as an impenetrable wall of flesh, with not a single vote for the plan coming from their ranks. And the only three Senators to cross the aisle were the two ladies from Maine, who in the privacy of their own homes are rumored to dress up as Democrats, and Arlen Specter, who pulled a Blagojevich, trading his support for inclusion of a pet project. But a good pet project. As opposed to all those bad pet projects. Which get called pork. By the pigs. Go figure.

In a courageous attempt to find common ground, Barack Obama risked infection from the mindless drones, meeting them en masse; yet not a single soul was able to summon the will to escape from the voodoo spell placed upon them by Rep. John Boehner (R-Hell). He's a powerful sorcerer who fuels his entranced hordes by reading aloud fragments of the sacred ancient texts of Ronald Reagan. No one knows how these pitiable wretches slid into these depths of depravity. It might have been their penchant for playing hardball and disinclination to don helmets.

Repelled by light and logic, with no thought for food, water, or self-preservation through long-range sustainable employment opportunities via shovel-ready infrastructure investment, the dull unthinking brainwashed shells sense their strength is in numbers and clutch together in a pack through Media-Land marching to the beat of a non-existent drummer. The most frightening aspect is not the glee they take in their current state, but how good they are at it. It's as if they were spawned to drag their feet.

But though the Chief Executive may have dodged the slow moving reanimated ghouls that are the Tax Cut Zombies from the Planet No! his learning curve has barely begun to arc. For soon he will inevitably encounter dark forces of equally if not more terrifying inhuman threats such as: the Lobbyist Vampires of Capitol Hill. American Werewolves in Baghdad. The Ethanol Children of the Corn. Nightmare on Wall Street. The Return of the Son of the Bride of Frankenstein's Social Security Meltdown. The Texas Oil Subsidies Chainsaw Massacre. The Night of the Living General Accounting Office Estimates. And Aliens 12,000,000. In Congress, no one can hear you negotiate.

**Highly Instructive ELECT TO LAUGH! Quote:** "Vote early and vote often." Al Capone.

# Man oh Man, I'm Mad

*A Teabagger's Lament.*

Man oh man, I'm mad. I'm mad as hell and I'm not going to take it anymore. Take what? I don't know. And that makes me mad too. Angry. Riled up. Cranky. Irate. Livid. Bellicose. Splenetic. Which has something to do with the spleen. Think it involves leakage. Whatever it is, it can't be good and I got it.

I'm mad at everything and everybody, but especially at career politicians. Not to mention career pediatricians. From now on, one of my kids gets sick, I'm taking them to see some incensed old coot straight off the street carrying a misspelled sign. Experience is way overrated. Why can't US Senator be an entry-level position?

I'm mad about paying taxes. Because... I don't like paying taxes. I'm tired of my hard earned money wasted on silly things like roads and air traffic controllers and paramedics and pipeline inspectors. And flossing. I hate that too. Who needs teeth? Members of the lamestream media elite, that's who. So they can lie through them. Those guys I'm mad at because they keep running stories about me being mad.

I'm mad at the government's nitpicking rules. Let corporations regulate themselves. They know what they're doing. I'm mad because I have to work two jobs just to get by and I'm mad rich people don't get more tax cuts. I'm mad about all the jobs that went overseas and I'm mad at unions demanding a living wage. I'm mad my life isn't better than my parents' and I'm mad I can't have everything now and force my children to pay for it. And knowing I'm confused just fuels my maddening.

I'm mad our Muslim President was born in Kenya. And don't bother me with your so-called facts. I know what I know and it makes me so mad I could just spit. So I do. Often. Right into the wind. And having the front of my shirt constantly moist, well, it don't make me happy.

I'm mad at both of the parties. All of the parties. Political parties and birthday parties and tailgate parties. I'm mad at Democrats because they're the polar opposite of mad and I'm mad at Republicans because they're not as mad as me. I'm so mad I'll bite off both my hands one finger at a time if that's what it takes. To prove I'm mad. Which I am.

I'm mad at immigrants for doing jobs that are beneath me. I'm mad at the French. I'm mad at French's mustard. I'm mad at people who put ketchup on hot dogs. I'm even mad at people who are mad at people who put ketchup on hot dogs. You can never hope to replicate the purity of my precious maditude.

Some folks don't ever get mad which makes me maddest of all. The hell is wrong with these people? These uppity madless ones. Oooh, they make me so mad. But they will be mad. Soon enough. Because my madness is going to bloom and grow until everyone is as mad as me. Which, is going to be tough. Because I'm really really mad. Did I mention I was mad? Good. Because I am. Mad, that is. Man oh man, I'm mad.

**Highly Instructive ELECT TO LAUGH! Quote:** "A low voter turnout is an indication of fewer people going to the polls." George W Bush

# Birther Bozos Need a New Nose

*Rationally realizing that this birther nonsense is far from over.*

Goaded into action by a nattering nabob of numbskulls, Barack Obama finally released the long form of his Certificate of Live Birth from the state of Hawaii, and hopefully threw the last shovel of dirt onto the grave of this inception nonsense, but the suspicion is... no. Probably not. As we speak, vanquished Birther Bozos are crawling out of the crypt searching for a new nose to wear. First the short form, now the long form, soon they'll want to see the director's cut. Then, on a television near you, the mini-series.

Anything to reinforce the strangeness of the first African American president. "Different than you and me." "Not a real American." Explains those silly cries of "We're taking our country back." Yeah. From the black guy.

We know what they really want. They want their water fountains and lunch counters and the fronts of their buses back. They want the 50s and "Leave it to Beaver" back. Ain't going to happen, angry old white guys. Barbara Billingsley is dead, man.

Don't think this is over. This is not over by a long shot. People believe what they want to believe. Facts be damned. 30% of the GOP still believes Saddam Hussein was responsible for 911 and weapons of mass destruction are currently cruising the streets of Fallujah disguised as ice cream trucks. Driven by men wearing tinfoil hats.

Obama's actions spurred some on the Right to charge him with orchestrating this whole distraction to keep the country from the real issues. Wow. The perfect somersault of blaming the hit and run victim for walking alone on a sidewalk late at night. "He attacked my bumper with his pelvis."

Others, like Newt Gingrich, refuse to be convinced. "There are still questions." Yeah, and besides, Obama's citizenship is due to a technicality, because on August 4th, 1961, Hawaii had been a state for less than two years. Maybe the flippo-units will switch tactics and demand proof he's not a Muslim. And won't be satisfied until they see a signed and dated parchment from Allah.

The disgrace is, the President was forced to hold a press conference, not to address the reshuffling of his national security team: but rather... where he was born. His exact quote was: "not going to be able to do our jobs if we get distracted by sideshows and carnival barkers." In response, the head carnival barker, Donald Trump, claimed to be honored for making the president jump through hoops like a trained Pomeranian. Who would also be ineligible to be president.

Donald is that kid in high school oblivious to the whole room including the teacher making fun of him. Faced with the very concrete evidence he insisted on viewing, you'd think he'd find a gracious way to back off, but you'd be as wrong as blaze orange camo. Cabernet Sauvignon in a can. Tinfoil condoms.

Instead, the Aerodynamic Coif upped the ante to question how a guy named Barack Hussein Obama got into Harvard Law and wants to see his college transcripts, which is a really, really sly way of throwing out the "n" word. Surprised he didn't use "shiftless" or "uppity."

Trump needs to show us samples of his DNA to prove he's actually a carbon-based life form. And where exactly was that thing on his head born? What's next: a mole count? Will a committee be empanelled to investigate the number of subcutaneous growths on the president's body? "Where are they and why is he hiding them? And exactly how many of them are shaped like his socialist supervisor, Cuba?"

**Highly Instructive ELECT TO LAUGH! Quote:** The great State of Mississippi has spurned Democrats and Republicans three times in the last 64 years, handing its electoral votes to racist third party candidates. Strom Thurmond in 1948, Harry Byrd in 1960, and George Wallace in 1968.

# The Care Less Party

*Vaulting back across the healthcare chasm on a really tall pole.*

All of America should drop to its knees and thank the GOP for providing us with replacement fireworks. As you undoubtedly are aware, cities all over the country this year were forced to cancel Fourth of July festivities due to fear of fire, glitchy computers, and twitchy bureaucrats. Like there's another kind.

The Republican House took great pains to salve our sensory deprived souls by trying to set off enough indoor fireworks to make the San Diego Big Bay Bust look like a fluttering votive candle. It was designed to be a spectacular explosion fueled by ego, obstinacy, and behavior so self-absorbed, the casual bystander might assume we were in the middle of an election year.

For the 33rd time, all House business slammed to a grinding halt to accommodate yet another vote to repeal Obama Care. Again. 33 times. Let's see what that looks like, shall we? 1. 2. 3. 4. 5. 6. 7. 8. 9. 10. 11. 12. 13. 14. 15. 16. 17. 18. 19. 20. 21. 22. 23. 24. 25. 26. 27. 28. 29. 30. 31. 32. 33.

You got to give the majority party credit for being able to flog this dead horse without getting any of the flying bits on them. 33 times is at least 32 times more than the administration ever tried to sell this bill to a public overwhelming in favor of its component parts.

They persevered even though everyone knows there's a better chance of flaming flamingos flying out of monkey butts than the Senate ever signing on. And getting past a Presidential veto, substitute polka dotted pterodactyls for the flamingos.

As political theater goes, this sad summer stock production fizzled with tired choreography and a script duller than Shakespeare in modern dress performed by 3rd graders in Mandarin. No wonder they keep trying to cut funding for the Arts, they're deathly afraid of the competition.

They rationalized this particular recycled Theater of the Absurd production by claiming a necessity to make a statement. And indeed a statement has been made. That Congress is broken and impotent and hopelessly in need of adult supervision. Even as we speak, you can hear their 8% approval rating clanking down the basement steps to unimagined depths.

It has been estimated this extended season of Cirque de Folly has taken up two cumulative weeks of business @ a cost of $24 million a week. That's what it takes to keep the congressional gears oiled and moving. Nearly $50 million to hammer home a point more tedious than slogging through the instruction booklet of an British made solar generator.

We're not even talking about more millions wasted to appease the base by blatantly restricting women's rights. This is all perfectly good money that could have been spent on further tax cuts for the rich. Even with inflation, fifty million dollars worth of oil subsidies could go a long way. Any idea how many car elevators you could buy with that kind of money?

The official Party Line on Obama Care is Repeal and Replace but nobody has anything to replace it with. Ask for specifics and Republicans mumble and fidget and get as vague as Donald Trump talking about the importance of ethics while closing the deal.

First there was Romney Care, and now we got Obama Care, but if the hard line conservatives get their way, this country is going to end up with We Don't Care. Less Care For You. Couldn't Care Less. Just might have to rename these fiscally responsible charlatans as… The Care Less Party.

**Highly Instructive ELECT TO LAUGH! Quote:** "I'm totally down with insurrection in the street. I've had a great time with that over the years. Insurrection in the voting booth is the other part of the equation." Jello Biafra.

Become a Hyperink reader. Get a special surprise.

Like the book? Support our author and leave a comment!

# V.

# The Democrats and Other Freaks of Nature

# Or... with friends like these...

Has to be the major problem with being a Democratic President. That whole democrat part. And the peculiar way your own party backs you up. Or to be more specific, doesn't. It all comes down to the very definition of the term "Liberal." According to the dictionary: it means "accepting of many viewpoints." Take the Occupy Movement. Please. Made a lot of sense and connected to people on a visceral level when they focused on Wall Street protesting greed and income inequality. But then the Global Warming people show up and you got to include them. Then Free Tibet wanders by and wants to set up a tent. And before you know it, the Hemp Contingent is selling t-shirts and rope belts. Then the Dolphin-Free Tuna people come a calling. And once they're in you *have* to let the Tuna-Free Dolphin folks in. Hey, no judgment. Of course the Sea Turtle People spent a lot of time and money on those costumes and they're going to wear them, damn it. And before you know it, the message has been diluted to where the black bloc takes over. I'm convinced that's why Democrats were so intent on passing the Stem Cell Bill. They're depending on that research to generate a spine. Here's some other choice observations on Barack's offensive line. Or lack thereof.

# Weinergate

*In which our intrepid correspondent trickily navigates the high road by addressing this messy situation with a figurative folded towel over his arm.*

Trust me. I really wanted to avoid the whole groin tweeting deal altogether but you might as well try to avert your eyes from a bullfight in a bowling alley backlit by fireworks. To the average civilian, the subject must seem riper than a three-week old banana for major mocking and scoffing and taunting. Slam-dunking from a step-ladder. The problem is: how do you mock a parody?

Unfortunately, the unfortunately named Anthony Weiner is the only game in town, sucking all the oxygen out of the newsroom. It's impossible to hear about Sarah Palin's newest Revisionist History Lesson. First, Paul Revere rang a bell to warn the British about gun control. What next? Abraham Lincoln declared war on the French to sabotage tort reform? Even the resignation of Newt Gingrich's entire campaign staff went relatively unnoticed. Apparently their love of this country is just too strong.

And this whole brouhaha is the New York Democrat's own damn fault. There wouldn't have been half the outcry if his name weren't a synonym for, among other things, sausage. After all, the choice of pronunciation is his. Could have taken a page out of the John Boehner playbook. Done the Boner/ Baner thing.

The Speaker of the House has 11 brothers and sisters. They're all Boners. He's the only Baner in the family. Seriously. His mother is a Boner. His father—well, 12 kids, you do the math.

And Weener could have gone with Whiner, which is still a lousy name for a politician. Apt for a Democrat, perhaps, but lousy nonetheless. Or he could have gone whole hog: "Yes, we spell it W-E-I-N-E-R, but it's pronounced... Schultz."

His singular consolation has to be his parents didn't add to his misery by christening him Harry. Or Richard. It's Anthony. Tony Weiner. Sounds like a high-class hot dog from a food truck in Marin. "2 Toney Wieners please." Or, the cartoon mascot in that animated short we all saw in 5th grade health class on the reproductive system. "Hi Kids! I'm Tony Wiener. Ready for a ride down the fallopian tube? Put your hard hats on. Let's go."

Congressman Weiner admitted sexting six different women he met online, including a porn star, who reported that he tried to get her to lie about their relationship, but she refused. Pretty sad when the porn industry exhibits higher standards of integrity than Congress. But that's old news.

So far, Weiner has resisted calls to step down, which has the Democratic leadership muttering unprintable imprecations under their breath. But the guy didn't break any laws. He's just a lout. And you can't force members of Congress to resign for being idiots or you'd never be able to assemble a quorum. "Let's see. what do we have today? Oaf. Cad. Fool. Lout. Creep. Toad. Buttwipe. Lizardstick. Ogre. Squeezebag. Thug. Vandal. Nimrod. Boehner. Johnson. Weiner. Bachmann. Sorry. Might want to try back tomorrow."

To say expressions of party support have been lacking is similar to noting that few Episcopal ministers sport flamboyantly inked barbed wire neck tattoos. Not even Bill Clinton spoke out in defense of his fellow serial womanizer. Bill Clinton, who officiated at Weiner's wedding. And doesn't that explain a lot? Amongst his other accomplishments we can now add to the former President's resume-carrier. Call him Typhoid Bubba. Then thank our lucky stars twitter capability wasn't available during his Administration.

**Highly Instructive ELECT TO LAUGH! Quote:** "Half of the American people never read a newspaper. Half never voted for President. One hopes it's the same half." Gore Vidal.

# My Two Cents

*Just a wee tiny bit of semi-friendly unsolicited advice for a struggling President.*

Only guessing, but a major problem with being President must be the people around you being more inclined to stick their face in a cast iron oscillating porch fan than tell you the unmitigated truth. Let's say you slip and fall and rip a hole in your pants down to your ankle while spilling scalding coffee on a little blind girl in a wheelchair in front of a nationally televised audience. The worst you could expect to hear from a staffer is "that could have gone better."

Therefore, it is my patriotic duty to offer up a little unsolicited advice intended for the President's Eyes Only. Yo. Barack. Dude. You should totally chill. And listen up. Why? Cuz this is the stuff Mister Chaff of Staff Rahm Emanuel can't tell you. And we won't go all ballistic on your butt or singe your receptionist's eardrums while doing it either.

First thing. Don't worry so much about the Republicans. They're going to do what they're going to do. You don't enter into the equation. Expect to be accused of everything. All the way from "done nothing at all" to "moved too quickly" and every permutation in between. At least you always know where these guys are coming from. From in front and behind and 160 different sides—all wielding knives of negativity.

It's your so-called friends you need to watch out for. The ones who smile and nod and laugh too loud at your jokes to cover the sound of the slip of a shiv between your third and fourth ribs on the left side. Trust me, with friends like these, you don't need Richard Shelby. Unfortunately, most of your buddies are Democrats. Which is a lot like saying most of a general's fighting force is terra cotta. The difference being terra cotta soldiers don't cut and run so fast they leave little puffs of cartoon smoke. And they all face in the same direction.

The second thing is, you need to develop an "or else." Work with you, or what?? Or Joe Biden sits next to you in the Congressional dining room every day for a week citing interstate trucking regulations while you try to eat? Lyndon Johnson plucked at the horsehair holding up the sword of Damocles for his "or else." Walk the line or find yourself whisked back to your home district as a clerk in Park and Rec's lost and found. His idea of compromise was letting you use his pen to sign your vow of allegiance.

Finally, your people have lost all sense of urgency. You got to fire somebody. You know—ax. Can. Dump. Sack. Pink slip. Terminate with extreme prejudice. Discharge. Unassign. 86. Downsize. Furlough. Ease out. Make redundant. Give the boot. Perform a bum's rush. Hand someone their marching orders. Assist in an accelerated career development shift. Impose a synergy related headcount restructuring. Heave a ho.

It doesn't matter who. Are you telling me in more than a year, nobody in the administration screwed up bad enough to be let go? Because if they haven't, you have. If you can't come up with an obvious target, pick someone at random. You really want to put the fear of god into Team Obama, get rid of Michelle. Or one of the kids. That's the best way of saying, "don't anybody want to get too complacent around here." Anyhow, that's our advice. No thanks necessary, we're here to help. First one's free.

**Highly Instructive ELECT TO LAUGH! Quote:** "If God had wanted us to vote, he would have given us candidates." Jay Leno.

# Pitchforks and Rainbows

*Investigating the grand gaping political chasms between the stubborn, the obdurate and the intransigent.*

America dodged the immediate damage of the killer Japanese tsunami but now a potentially more dangerous phenomenon threatens to wash across our nation. The new political paradigm—concrete intransigency. No quarter asked for—no quarter given. Us versus Them, and Us is me, and whoever likes me. The Colosseum reborn in the Senate. I'm so right and you're so wrong that anybody who agrees with you deserves to be publicly assaulted and abused and eaten by lions.

Say what you will about the Liberals, for the most part, they believe deep down in their bones that impoverished kids enrolled in Head Start programs can contribute to society and make the world a better place to live. For all of us. And rich people should pay for that. Conservatives wonder why these kids don't pull themselves up by their bootstraps the way they did when daddy bequeathed them their first oil well. Life is a race and anybody with a Head Start is cheating. Anybody not part of their immediate family, that is.

These basic attitudes stem from deep-rooted philosophical differences. The Liberal idea is "by helping the greater good, it will eventually come back and benefit me." While Conservatives believe exactly the opposite. "By helping me, it will eventually come back and benefit me." And even conservatives laugh at that line, because they don't care.

Now that politics is a 24/7 media proposition, those positions have calcified like petrified wood. Conservative voices dominating center stage today live in a black and white land where compromise equals defeat and discussion means you taking notes while they talk. The liberal world is a rainbow of colors where the government provides everyone with that big box of 64 crayons encouraging them to write on the walls. Anybody's walls.

Liberals want to nurture the brotherhood of man while Conservatives deem this mythical brotherhood just another left wing conspiracy trying to separate them from their money. Conservatives sincerely believe they stole all their stuff fair and square, while Liberals think people with too much stuff should be required to give some of their stuff to people who don't have any stuff. Problem is absolutely nobody considers their collection of stuff to be too much.

Liberals want to reform prisoners. Conservatives don't believe in taking any. Liberals would rather lose honorably than be accused of acting unseemly. As a matter of fact, Liberals are more comfortable losing than they are winning. Conservatives will do whatever it takes to win, including telling kids their teachers are the enemy. Not only are conservatives bad losers, they're sore winners as well.

Another odd thing is both sides continue to play the game under different narratives. Liberals act like associate producers at a folk fair trying to choreograph the welcoming dance of converging cultures failing to notice the ragged band of Conservatives lighting torches and running headlong towards them up the castle hill armed with pitchforks.

There's a war going on but only one side is aware of it. You'd think the surprise attack that went down in Wisconsin would be the sharp poke in the side necessary to wake up Liberals. But knowing them, they're more concerned with strengthening the guardrails on the castle hill road and introducing legislation to reform pitchfork safety standards. "You should put corks on those."

**Highly Instructive ELECT TO LAUGH! Note:** Barack Obama is our 44th president, right? Well, kind of. America has only had 43 different Presidents. Grover Cleveland served two non-consecutive terms and is counted as our 22nd and 24th Presidents.

# Crouching Lurkers

*Gazing into the debt-crisis crystal ball and unsurprisingly receiving a busy signal.*

Run for the hills everybody! Armageddon is imminent! The sky is beyond falling; it's anvil plummeting! Onto our heads so fast, clouds are whistling the love theme from the movie "2012." The US economy is about to meltdown like a popsicle left on a Palm Springs picnic table, and it's only a matter of time before this country liquefies into Greece's financial twin without the pleasant distraction of all that melodious zither music.

Seniors and sick people and soldiers are destined to be tossed into the streets to battle mutant rats for food. The 3 branches of the government will inevitably be deemed too expensive, and we'll be forced to let one go. All hell is about to break loose. Don't you get it? We're doomed! Doomed!! Then again... maybe not.

What *is* clear, is nothing. Here's what we kind of, almost, pretty much, but not quite know for sure: Unless Congress agrees to raise the Debt Ceiling, America's authority to borrow money will expire and the government may or mayn't shut down. What *that* means, nobody knows. Could be not so good or it could be really really bad or it could be stick your head between your knees and kiss your butt goodbye bad.

And yes, I can hear you whispering, "hey, schmucko, shutting down the government doesn't sound half bad to me. About time we kicked those freakin' freeloaders off of the dole." Point well taken. But understand—the responsibility for those big red "Freeloader" stickers you're so anxious to plaster on foreheads will not be given to you. It will be handed from one government bureaucrat to another government bureaucrat, which means your forehead could easily end up sporting a collection of big red stickers. Don't ever forget—one man's pork is another man's hickory smoked bacon bits.

Both parties love striding histrionically across the stage pronouncing in loud mellifluous tones how proud and determined they are to stick to their core principles while demanding the other side compromise. The theory being the other side is more likely to abandon core principles because, let's be honest, they aren't really core principles at all, so much as they are re-election talking points. And you know what, they're right. Which side? Exactly!

The Republicans are demanding cuts in entitlement programs, which the President said he'd consider. The Democrats have in their own inimitable roundabout way brought up the possibility of maybe raising taxes on a few rich people, which Eric Cantor, the Under Speaker of the House, says he won't consider. Ever. Never ever.

And that, my friends, is where we stand. Although the word "stand" might be affording the participants a wee bit too much credit. Squirm. Slink. Skulk. Dodge. Creep. Crouch. Lurk. Loiter. Weasel. Cower. Any of which might be more apropos.

Unfortunately, this is, was, and forever shall be, the way of all things in Congress. Much hollow bluster and empty fury in a noisy gamble to appease the base until it becomes crystal clear whom the general populace (Independents) blames for the gridlock, then everyone quickly signs something nobody likes and both parties walk off declaring victory. Think of it as the Vietnamization of Congressional negotiation. No peace at all and very little honor.

**Highly Instructive ELECT TO LAUGH! Quote:** "It's not who votes that counts, it's who counts the votes." Joseph Vissarionovich Stalin.

Like the book? Support our author and leave a comment!

# VI.

# Issues. Issues. Issues.

# Or... we got your issues right here.

Remember back in grade school, when all learning came to a screeching halt while the teacher stopped to explain what was going on to the unruly kids? She'd spend an entire morning trying to simplify the lesson plan so they could understand it. Using small words in her annoyingly patient voice, which tended to pitch strident the slower she spoke. Well, that's what's happened to America. We're being held hostage by the dim. People used to be embarrassed to be stupid. Now they're walking around all proud and stuff wearing their density like some sort of badge of authenticity. Waving misspelled signs and talking such a pack of nonsense you'd think syphilitic monkeys had crawled up their butts and were blowing "Oh Suzanna" on perforated livers. During the health care riots, Newsweek photographed a guy with a sign that read; "Stop Socializing USA & Keep Youre Hands Off My Medicare." Dude. That's two different signs. Of course, easy to figure out why this guy is so opposed to health care; he's obviously intimate with the failures of our public education system. But I digress. And that wasn't the only issue that reared its ugly head. Although, there's no time to talk about pirates. Wanted to talk about the pirates. Oh well.

# Saint Taxes

*Floating a modest proposal.*

The government has it all wrong. Yeah, yeah, I know. Who's ever heard THAT before? What next? "This Just In! Fire is Hot. Water: Reputed to be Wet!" Will tell you what's got my knickers in a big old knotted ball the size of Kobe Bryant's ego on Jupiter this time around is the age-old practice of politicians balancing their financial shortsightedness on the backs of the little guy. The little BAD guy. I'm talking about Sin Taxes. And mayhaps be secreting a bit more outrage than the rest of you good folk, since I'm pretty much that little bad guy everybody is talking about.

Oh yeah, I'm bad. To the bone. I drink and I smoke and I eat red meat. Often. Not sweets so much, but make up for it with the savories. Cheetos? Doritos? Kettle Brand Salt and Fresh Ground Pepper Krinkle Cut potato chips? Indeedy-do. Betcha can't eat one. Bag. And what drives me nuttier than the pecan pie shelf at an Interstate truck stop in Georgia is the self-righteous attitude these pillars of the community adopt while squeezing folks like me tighter than a nickel in a vise grips.

We Sin Tax Targets aren't allowed to squawk either, because, well… we're sinners. We're expected to quietly cower in our damp greasy smoky donut crumb littered corner of the basement as they slap and gouge us for doing that which every 4th grader knows oughtn't be done. Like pouring stuff into our bodies that is used to wash the rust off of chrome bumpers. For cupping our hands over our ears making la-la-la noises whenever a nutritionist pops up on the television. And possessing less impulse control than a mountain lion in a fish market post closing time.

It may seem short term tempting, but I'm convinced these new liquor, cigarette and sodie pop surcharges are entirely the 180 degrees wrong way to go. It's a scientific fact that we degenerate miscreant reprobates kick off early. Hardly manage to crawl into our sixties. Every time I eat, I can hear my arteries harden. That's what the government should want. We aren't the ones sucking up all the Social Security and Medicare money. It's you damn sproutheads that linger.

That's why I propose; instead of Sin Taxes, we go the other way entirely, and institute a series of Saint Taxes. Holistic tariffs. Longevity levies. You want to live forever? Fine: pay for it. Ante up Mofo.

From now on, every piece of fresh fruit requires a prescription.

Tiramisu is subsidized.

Cholesterol credits can be purchased, sold, and traded.

Discount potato chip coupons are included on the bottom of your 1040 form.

Asparagus, sunblock, and yoga are illegal.

The higher your blood pressure, the lower your taxes.

Every six months you have to renew your seat belt license.

French fries and cigarettes are handed out for free like government cheese.

Beer drinkers receive rebates for every six-pack.

Joggers have to pay tolls based on GPS readouts in their shoes.

Water fountains are replaced with salt licks.

The only way to score tofu is from waitresses in jazz clubs.

Fried Chicken is known as Vitamin C.

And finally, you can waltz into any bar in the country for free but are charged incredible amounts of money every time you even talk about seeing a doctor.

This paradigm shift should be easy to implement, especially since those last couple are already in place.

**Highly Instructive ELECT TO LAUGH! Quote:** "When I was young, I was told anybody could become president. Now I'm beginning to believe it." Clarence Darrow.

# It's My Money

*Exhibiting a certain pride for suppressing my banking frustration to something under scalding rage.*

Ah. October. Patio umbrellas down. Storm windows up. The turning of the leaves. The crisping of our ears. Playoff baseball. Halloween just a few weeks off. We'll get back to the most bracing month a bit later, but first a few words about the recent decision by major banks to charge customers 5 bucks a month to use ATM cards for routine purchases. And those few words are "You Greedy Stinking Ravenous Money-Grubbing Avaricious Pigs."

How much money do you have to make? I mean I get it. You are not non-profit organizations. Few of us are. Advertently. Your task is to find new ways to make more moolah. Same here. You just happen to be a whole lot better at it than the rest of us. And with the scratch to rewrite the rules, the skids get greased in your favor. Good for you. But do you really need all the greenbacks? Every single dime? All the dough? Really?

What were your profits last year? Like a bazilliondy dollars? Isn't that enough? Do stockholders require double-digit returns every quarter? Incredibly foolish to expect hubris after causing the worst financial crisis in 80 years, but wouldn't it be wiser to leave behind a couple of bucks for the rest of us? You know, so we can do business with you. Commerce. Otherwise you'll have all the capital, no customers and be forced to restrict all your interactions to other banks, and trust me, you're not going to like that.

Or is that the ultimate goal? To gather all the money in the world, becoming a money museum? Then we pony up pretty colored stones just to look at the money we no longer have. And you know what happens then. You make it your mission to control the world's supply of pretty colored stones. Go ahead. We'll switch to short smooth pointy sticks.

This is not your money we're talking about. This is my money. You supposed to pay me for your use of my money. That's the deal. What's the interest rate on savings accounts now, .02%? Oh right, the fed is maintaining artificially low interest rates to boost economic climes. But shouldn't that mean the interest rate on my credit cards goes down too? I'm paying 30%. In some states that's usury. For crum's sake, you can strike a better deal on the street with Vinnie.

Nickel and diming us to death? Hah! Those were the good old days. Now you're squeezing every penny so hard Lincoln's head is starting to squirt liquid copper. There's a charge for using a teller. A charge for not using a teller. A charge for telling the teller where to stick the charge. "Convenience fees" from our friendly neighborhood financial institutions. Use a rival bank and the charges get doubled or tripled or whatever "ed" you call times 36. What are those? Infidelity fees?

Don't you get it? It's My Money. We're not talking about credit cards where I pay you to lend me some quick cash. These are automatic deductions from an account into which I have already placed ample coin of the realm. MY MONEY! Keep your filthy paws off my money, you damn stinking apes. Wow. Sorry. As you can see, I'm a bit ambivalent on this one. What? Oh yeah. October. October sucks.

**Highly Instructive ELECT TO LAUGH! Quote:** "Votes are like trees. If you are trying to build a forest. if you have more trees than you have forests, then at that point the pollsters will probably say you will win." Dan Quayle.

# Kooky Kabuki Terrain

*Wondering if the politicians are making business crazy or if the craziness is making the business political.*

This health care thing has driven people crazier than Johnny Depp in a Max Fleischer cartoon on acid. Pro or con, your rhetoric better be cranked up to eleven and soaring past the outer orbit of Neptune's third moon, or you're going to be as invisible as a tax collector with a soggy paper plate full of Swedish meatballs sitting next to the deceased at a wake.

Talk show host Rush Limbaugh jumped into this peculiar March Madness feet first, threatening to leave the US should health care reform pass. He must realize for a lot of folks, that's a big win-win. If the prospect of his permanently playing ex-pat doesn't motivate progressives, nothing will. He even mentioned Costa Rica as a possible destination. Where they have universal heath care. Just like every industrialized country in the world. Although your access to Oxycontin may vary.

Eric Massa, the New York Democrat who admitted grabbing a staffer's staff, embarked on a media based whining tour charging he was hounded out of office by the White House and smeared because of his opposition to health care reform. But even though he was willing to speak ill of the Administration, Glenn Beck washed his hands of Tickle-Me-Eric, after the former Congressman trotted out some intra-personal top bunk Naval snorkeling documentation. When a pissed off Democrat is too far gone for Glenn Beck, things truly have escalated into kooky Kabuki terrain.

Meanwhile, in another part of town, Senator Orrin Hatch railed that if Democrats try to jam a health care bill through Congress it will destroy bipartisanship. Oh no! Not that! Talk about killing the dodo. Apparently this guy is more worried about dead fantasies than sick Americans. Then Senator Mitch McConnell ratcheted up the exponential wackiness by warning Democrats they face Electoral Armageddon in the fall, which isn't fair; like regaling 6 year old girls with tales of the hairy spiders that live under their bed before saying "sleep tight."

Obama, his own self, can be found careening around the country like an over-caffeinated Chihuahua engaged in a last ditch effort to sell the bill to what you might call his hesitant posse. Yeah. Recalcitrant Democrats. What are the odds? Like calling a flash flood-irksome. Hell, at this point Obama would be happy to pass anything. Health care. The jobs bill. A hook pattern. Kidney stone. A Volkswagen Van.

The overwhelming discombobulating apprehension is that the President isn't just piloting his own kamikaze fighter into the carrier of health care, he's taking all his troops with him on the same suicide mission. One that will make Gallipoli look like a weekend pass at an Istanbul brothel. After all, it's not his butt on the re-election line this fall, and the GOP strategy to stall any and or all proceedings has frothed Democratic incumbents into such a lather, the sweat dripping off their faces is shorting out microphones all across this great land of ours.

Now we're hearing the target passage date might be a bit more elastic than the waistband of a RINO's tutu. The good news is sooner or later, this bill will either become law or not become law and everybody can settle back down to their normal routine of accusation, obfuscation, and procrastination until election day. But until then, better keep taking your vitamins; this protracted health care debate seems to have a side effect. Its making a lot of people sick.

**Highly Instructive ELECT TO LAUGH! Quote:** "It's easy being a humorist when you have the whole government working for you." Will Rogers

# Pity the Poor Rich

*Defending those fortunate fraught folks F. Scott Fitzgerald famously framed as being different from you and me.*

Allow me to offer up a few words in defense of one of the most maligned groups in America today. Citizens, who through a simple twist of fate, are routinely subjected to some of the most scathing condemnation and slanderous stereotyping in the annals of recorded history. Of course I'm talking about those unsung heroes of capitalism, the highly lubed pistons in the engine of our economy: the rich.

Isn't it time we stopped demonizing the wealthy simply because they have a couple more bucks than the rest of us? You've heard all the scurrilous charges: Greedy. Selfish. Thieving. Insatiable. Rapacious. Grasping. Power-mad. Heartless. Hog-like. Wear a lot of pink. And what's the deal with the no socks thing? Like they can't afford them?

People, settle down. The rich are just like the rest of us, only with access to a better class of orthodontists. They put their Egyptian silk trousers on one leg at a time, same as you and me. Besides, wasn't it God, in the Bible, who said money can't buy you happiness? Although admittedly, it can be used as barter for a lot of stuff that might make you happy: like prescription drugs and bus fare and rent and ramen.

Being rich isn't all a bed of roses, you know. It isn't easy having green. You can't trust anybody. That includes but is not limited to—perfect strangers, casual acquaintances, prospective suitors, family members, non-profit organizations, banks, shysters, crooks, and lawyers, but I repeat myself, not to mention the most dangerous threat of all, other rich people. Do the names Bernie Madoff, Warren Buffett, and the Kardashian Crime Family have any meaning here?

Off-shore accounts can be sooooooo confusing. The cost of private jet fuel is legalized extortion. And good housekeeping help is impossible to find. Scoundrels constantly plot to make your money, their money. Hence, rich people are forced to cower in a continual state of paranoia. But like buttery soft vicuna sport coats, it comes with the territory. Nobody robs poor people. Well, actually, rich people rob poor people, but that's different. That's business.

The main problem with being rich is never having enough money. And while liberals gripe and snipe that the rich and their corporations are sitting on trillions (no, really, trillions) of dollars waiting for the "correct political climate" to rehire workers, the fact that they employ hundreds of thousands of lawyers to ferret out loopholes to keep from paying taxes goes criminally unreported. It's all about jobs, people.

I know what you're saying, "how can you defend these avaricious squeezebags? These scabrous zits on the forehead of egalitarianism? These predatory pus wads with the principles of diseased weasels in heat." Well, self-preservation mostly; because someday, like everybody else in this grand land of ours, I intend to be rich. A major reason why Democrats find it impossible to wage a class war.

The difference is, I'd be a really good rich person. Would cheerfully pay my *fair share* of taxes and regularly engage the little people in sparkling conversation and never stiff waiters or prostitutes no matter how lousy the service received. How rich? Filthy rich. Rich enough not to stuff the Kleenex box in my suitcase when I check out of hotel rooms. I'd leave it right there on the bathroom sink for the next guy. It's a goal.

**Highly Instructive ELECT TO LAUGH! Quote:** "Just received the following wire from my generous Daddy. 'Dear Jack. Don't buy a single vote more than necessary. I'll be damned if I'm going to pay for a landslide.'" JFK.

# Back in the Fold

*We didn't tell you to wear red in the woods.*

Give Congress the benefit of the doubt and say they do work out a compromise on the debt ceiling extension. This country could still slip into default, and then you know what happens—We'll have to move back in with England. Who's going to be happy then? Nobody. You think it's embarrassing slinking home after college, try waiting 236 years.

Already dreading the dressing down we'll be forced to patiently endure should we make it through the front door. "Well, well, well, look who's back. Couldn't hack it on our own, could we, 'Mister I'm Ready for Independence?' Not much bloody fun being labeled a fading superpower, now is it boyo?

Notice you didn't rush right over to your good friend China's house. What's the matter, have a fight with your new BFF? Or do they want some of their money back? What about Egypt? Don't they owe you a bit of something? Or did you already squander it away like your post 911 goodwill? Typical.

So. I suppose you'll be wanting your old room back. Well, forget about it. Pakistan has been renting that room for almost three decades. Very tidy people. And quiet. Too quiet, if you ask me. But they cook. All the time. Nice break for your mother. Bit smelly in the kitchen with all those spices, but quite tasty really.

What is wrong with you? Why can't you manage your money better like your younger brother Canada? Yes, a bit stodgy perhaps, but nose to the grindstone, that's Canada in a nutshell. Still respect their Royals. Not like you or that drunken lout Australia. Don't get me started. Does the term Diamond Jubilee have any meaning to you? Didn't think so.

This is totally against my better judgment, but your mother says you can crash on the basement couch. Just for a couple of weeks, mind you. And this isn't the Ritz. While you live in this house, you will live by our rules, mister. That means the telly shuts off at 10pm. Sharp. And yes, there's only 4 channels. Stop whingeing.

No more making fun of the Queen. You hear me? And get this through your thick little skull, health care is free. For everybody. That's right. Stitches may be a bit larger than you're used to, but I dare say you'll get accustomed to it.

One last thing, no more wars. Look at me when I'm talking to you. If I hear of one more scrape you've gotten yourself into, you'll be back on the street so fast it'll make Barack Obama's head spin. Faster. Nobody wants you mucking about with your sticky little fingers in their business anymore. Do we understand each other? Good.

Now get your big butt downstairs and wash up. Put on a tie. Supper's at 5. Doesn't look like you've missed many meals. And while you're down there, clean up a spot under the stairwell, there's a clever lad. Ireland just called. They're on their way over."

**Highly Instructive ELECT TO LAUGH! Quote:** "Democracy is a form of government that substitutes election by the incompetent many for appointment by the corrupt few." George Bernard Shaw.

# The 2012 Political Animal Awards

**BEST COSTUME:** Rick Santorum for that winning period look—hearkening back to a young Mr. Rogers with rabies.

**BAD TIMING AWARD:** Tim Pawlenty, for deserting the Presidential line-up before getting his own shot at leading the pack. Runner-Up. Mitch Daniels.

**UNCLEAR ON THE CONCEPT AWARD:** Herman Cain, for continuing to blame the media for discovering his fan full of feces.

**THE DUMBER THAN HE ALREADY LOOKS AWARD:** In an extremely competitive field, Rick Perry.

**THE NOT AS DUMB AS HIS HAIR LOOKS AWARD:** For the 6th consecutive year, Donald Trump.

**THE CLAUDE RAINES INVISIBLE MAN AWARD:** George W Bush.

**BEST SUPPORTING ACTRESS:** In a thankless role, Calista Gingrich.

**THE WE CAN'T FIND A MUZZLE BIG ENOUGH AWARD:** Joe Biden. May have to retire this award in his name.

**THE WHY WON'T ANYONE RETURN MY CALLS AWARD: DEMOCRATIC DIVISION:** John Edwards. John Kerry. Anthony Weiner.

**THE WHY WON'T ANYONE RETURN MY CALLS AWARD: REPUBLICAN DIVISION:** Dick Cheney. Pat Robertson. Glenn Beck.

**BEST SPECIAL EFFECTS:** Industrial Light & Magic for making Mitt Romney appear so lifelike.

**BEST MAKE UP:** Newt Gingrich for his very convincing Walking Dead grimace.

**BEST CHOREOGRAPHY:** Grover Norquist.

**THE "OH MY GOD, NOT YOU AGAIN" AWARD:** Whoever decided contraception made for a good election year wedge issue.

**BEST BOY:** Marcus Bachmann.

**BEST ANIMATION:** Chris Christie.

**BEST NEWCOMER:** Paul Ryan for his controversial scripts, "Roadmap for America's Future," & "Path to Prosperity."

**THE LUCKY IT WASN'T BITTEN OFF AWARD:** Arizona Governor Jan Brewer.

**THE HOW CAN WE MISS YOU IF YOU WON'T GO AWAY AWARD:** Ron Paul.

**BEST ENSEMBLE IN A MUSICAL OR COMEDY:** The entire Republican Party Presidential Nomination cast.

**BEST ACTOR:** Body of work award goes to Speaker of the House John Boehner for various portrayals as outraged defender of fiscal responsibility, obstinate party stalwart, and sophisticated gentleman to whom gracious cooperation is of the highest priority and doing it all while implausibly orange.

**BEST DIRECTION:** The Koch Brothers.

**THE BETTER TO BE LUCKY THAN GOOD AWARD:** Barack Obama.

**Highly Instructive ELECT TO LAUGH! Quote:** "The difference between a democracy and a dictatorship is that in a democracy you vote first and take orders later; in a dictatorship you don't have to waste your time voting." Charles Bukowski.


Become a Hyperink reader. Get a special surprise.

Like the book? Support our author and leave a comment!

# VII.

# The Republican Primary Field Primer

# Or... when weird things happen to loud people.

It was more exciting than a zip-line over crocodile infested streams watching the Republican Reality show that played across television screens the last 18 months. The entertaining miniseries was a huge ratings blockbuster. But like a typical JJ Abrams production; murky and confusing. The GOP plot line meandered more than a scampering toddler in the horse barns of the North Dakota State Fair. Think third year of Twin Peaks. And make it foggier. Another stumbling block was the format. What exactly was this thing? A game show, a mockumentary or a sit-com sponsored by Planters to capitalize on all the mixed nuts involved? Proctor & Gamble should thrown their name onto the proceedings because of how deep we entered soap opera territory. And everybody got a shot at leading the polls. Some said they were scraping the bottom of the barrel? Noooo, they were squeezing the goo from between the slats that leaked out of the bottom of the barrel. Pat Robertson said that the field of Republican candidates was too extreme. Pat Robertson said that. Which is like having your drug intervention hosted by Lindsay Lohan. And Charlie Sheen is driving the van. But it was entertaining.

# Frequently Asked Questions About the Iowa Caucuses

*Answering a few common queries concerning the left ventricle of the Heartland.*

**Q.** A little help here. Exactly what are the Iowa Caucuses?

**A.** The Iowa Caucuses *is* a method of choosing a presidential nominee. Held every 4 years. Usually in Iowa.

**Q.** Why is *it* so important?

**A.** Number one in the batting order. Opening stanza of an epic poem. The recorded preamble to the Republican Nomination Symphony is over, and the citizen orchestra is about to play.

**Q.** What?

**A.** Gentlemen, start your engines.

**Q.** What precisely happens?

**A.** Nobody knows. The process is sort of like musical chairs without the chairs. And no music.

**Q.** How did this get started?

**A.** It began with early Iowans throwing small round ruinish stones into hollowed out stumps, which were placed atop cast iron kettles brimming with pig entrails— then the omens interpreted by a circle of community elders wearing ceremonial necklaces of hand-carved stringed chestnuts.

**Q.** And when did it transform into the current method?

**A.** Actually, its still pretty much the same.

**Q.** How is a caucus different than a primary?

**A.** For the Republicans, not much. For Iowan Democrats it means that people don't vote. They attend. Huddle with like minded others in designated candidate corners, but if not enough people join your posse, your group is disbanded and everybody wanders around in search of a second or third choice. So supporters who corner the breath mint and deodorant market hold a huge advantage.

**Q.** Might there be worse ways in choosing a candidate than picking the one with the best smelling supporters?

**A.** Oh yes indeed. Look at North Korea.

**Q.** How's my good buddy Jon Huntsman doing these days?

**A.** Little green around the gills. Polling around 1% with a margin of error of 4%. So he could very well end up owing Iowa a couple delegates.

**Q.** How believable are the polls?

**A.** Don't bet the farm. Iowans are a fierce stubborn people. They don't call them Buckeyes or Hawkeyes or Hoosiers or whatever they call them for nothing you know.

**Q.** What are you saying?

**A.** That folks in Iowa love to confound conventional wisdom by throwing in with the underdog. Can we say Ron Paul in a squeaker?

**Q.** Why Iowa?

**A.** Why not Iowa?

**Q.** No, I mean why does a state that Minnesotans make fun of, get to go first?

**A.** Who do you want to go first: Louisiana? California? Texas? American Somoa?

**Q.** Your point being?

**A.** At least Iowa is representative.

**Q.** Of white people.

**A.** In the form of a question, please.

**Q.** Okay, how diverse is Iowa?

**A.** White, white, white, white, white, white, white. Whiter than a "Justin Bieber Christmas in Norway Special." Mashed potatoes on paper plates with a side of cauliflower white.

**Q.** You call that representative?

**A.** It is a Republican affair.

**Q.** Point taken. Who can participate?

**A.** Anybody who pre-registers as a Republican. And brings snacks.

**Q.** Does it cost anything to participate?

**A.** Just the tiniest piece of your soul.

**Q.** How are caucuses better than primaries?

**A.** Well, they're a whole lot more fun to say. Try it in a sentence: "I slipped on the ice and broke my caucuses."

**Q.** What happens in Iowa on January 4th when the circus packs up and moves to New Hampshire?

**A.** Iowa radio stations will stop screaming about treason and hypocrisy and go back to hog futures and herbicidal ads; just the way God intended.

**Highly Instructive ELECT TO LAUGH! Quote:** "We'd all like to vote for the best man, but he's never on the ballot." Frank McKinney.

# Republican Primary Angry Birds

- Little red bird that squawks a lot but doesn't affect much of anything. Herman Cain.

- Yellow bird that can break through load bearing walls. Ron Paul.

- Weird green bird with boomerang action, aping almost perfectly the parabolic arc that is his coif. Donald Trump.

- Big lumpy white bird that drops exploding eggs, Michele Bachmann.

- Little blue bird that splits into three little blue birds at the touch of the screen; Texas king of multiple personalities, Rick Perry.

- Big red bird with all the subtlety of a cliff-plummeting anvil whose only skill is to destroy everything in its path. Newt Gingrich.

- Bird that is not a bird at all, but a bomb whose fuse is triggered by touching any object: Rick Santorum.

- Mighty Eagle. Special order bird pummels entire screen to bits, but you have to pay a little extra. Mitt Romney.

Next, we investigate the eerie resemblance between the Supreme Court and Doodle Jump.

**Highly Instructive ELECT TO LAUGH! Note:** 80% of all computer ballots in the country are counted by two companies. Diebold and ES&S. The President of ES&S and the vice president of Diebold are brothers.

# Red Meat Slam Dance

*Where the criminally uncommunicative pay homage to the Great Communicator.*

A full complement of Republican presidential candidates gathered for the Battle Royale at the Ronald Reagan Library in Seamy (Simi) Valley, California. Though only there in spirit, the Great Communicator could have supplied power for the entire proceedings had the networks harnessed him spinning in his grave like a rotisserie chicken in the middle of a power surge.

The 8 challengers for his glass slipper didn't just break the Gipper's 11th Commandment, "Thou shall not speak ill of other Republicans," they stomped on it with football cleats and shoved it down a sewer grate with a broken rake handle. It was a red meat, power-tie slam dance with operatic overtones.

Anticipation ran higher than Charlie Sheen on New Year's Eve in Las Vegas that a hockey match might break out and the blood thirsty audience was not going to be satisfied until lecterns dripped with copious spillage. Before Rick Perry could answer Brian Williams' question about the execution of 234 inmates on his watch, the crowd erupted into applause like emeritus alumni at an Assassins State University homecoming. Creeping the moderator out more than pinworms in the bottom of his footie pajamas.

The contestants proved their bona fides competing to see who most disliked the president. "Oh yeah, well, I really really hate him." "He's worse than PBS Pledge Drives." "Responsible for all evil worldwide throughout history and into perpetuity."

Eyes on the prize, Newt Gingrich cautioned panel mates to keep the attacks focused on Obama, while castigating the media for trapping them in this internecine warfare. The rest of the contingent dismissed his admonition like a group of Oakland Raider tailgaters suffering through an elderly aunt's opinions on blitz protection. Newt Gingrich—the soul of reason. Something has gone horribly awry.

We learned Michele Bachmann believes in $2 a gallon gasoline and "a strong bold leader who will lead," and that she spent the last three weekends going to restaurants and thinks drilling for oil in the Everglades is a good idea. So, apparently she's orchestrating an electoral strategy that disincludes Florida's mighty 27.

Rick Perry hates cancer and called Social Security "a Ponzi scheme," not once, but three times, so Florida is obviously not on his front burner either. Arch-enemy to all things science, Perry supported his "climate change, what climate change" philosophy by comparing himself to Galileo. You can't make stuff up like this.

Ron Paul has been mauled by the TSA and is not happy about it. Or much of anything else. Also, we now know it is virtually impossible for Willard Mitt Romney to be out-smugged by anybody, even an unctuous Texan. Hermann Cain likes Chile. The country, not the food. And the major difference between Elvis Presley and Rick Santorum's candidacy is… there is none, they're both rock-salt, shaved-dust, dead.

Jon Huntsman may be running for the wrong party's nomination. Trying to steer the group from the edge of various abysses, he and Newt shared the big boy babysitter role, while Bachmann lost more momentum than a dark matter anvil hitting a freeway sound wall. Big winner… Sarah Palin. For being prescient enough to not to have made up her mind yet.

But there's plenty of time. This was just the premier stop for the traveling abattoir. There are dozens of chances for continued bloodletting until either Perry or Romney drops from the death of 1000 cuts, or they take each other out in a murder-suicide pact. Meanwhile Team Obama roots for Perry from the sidelines the same way Jimmy Carter cheered on the honorary host and Bonzo's sidekick back in 80. Another teachable moment: be careful what you wish for.

**Highly Instructive ELECT TO LAUGH! Quote:** "Anti-intellectualism has been a constant thread winding its way through our political and cultural life, nurtured by the false notion that democracy means that 'my ignorance is just as good as your knowledge." Issac Asimov.

# GOP Pledge Drive

*Vowing to make the pledging pledgers make no more pledges save Lemon.*

I pledge. You pledge. We all pledge. Pledge allegiance to the flag. Pledge to stop smoking and drinking...so much... in front of the kids... on Tuesdays. Pledge to lose weight. We're pledging fools. NPR and PBS are ridiculous with their annoying pledge drives. Our leaders pledge and pledge and pledge to stop ignoring the past. Then they don't. And in every other living room in America you can smell Lemon Pledge. These are the pledges of our lives.

But this campaign season, the pledging thing has rocketed out of control with leaky hydraulics and broken O-rings. Gotten to where anybody who plans on getting up close and personal with a Republican candidate in the near future might want to carry an oath-repelling umbrella because pledges are raining down like frog parts after a methane gas explosion in the amphibian wing of an aquarium.

The pledges have become longitudinally rampant, running all over the map from gay marriage to abortion to Shariah law to the teaching of intelligent design. Which most of us agree is neither. Keep waiting for the American Association of Apple Growers to issue its demand that potential nominees publicly vow to avoid blueberry pies while running for president. "Communists eat cherry pie." "Meringue is so French." "Rhubarb is for Obama Care Loving Wussies."

Rick Perry recently signed the Anti-Gay Marriage Pledge, which counteracts his previous pledge to leave the question up to the states. So, according to him, pandering to homophobia trumps states rights. Of course Rick Perry not so long ago pledged not to run for President, so he seems to have a rather fluid attitude as far as these pledges go. This good ol' boy needs to be careful lest he get labeled a pledging contradicter.

Righter than right conservatives first gained success with the Susan B. Anthony Pledge in which anybody running for president promises to appoint antiabortion cabinet members. Then out flew the Cut, Cap, and Balance Pledge, which cuts, caps, and balances the budget, focusing on giving rich people more money. So it can trickle down to us.

And now, the Marriage Vow, which is similar to, yet tactically different from the Anti-Gay

Marriage Pledge. In this, candidates oppose same sex marriage, reject Shariah Law, and pledge personal fidelity to their spouse. Which you'd think they'd have done during their wedding, but you never know with these crazy kids and their oddball vows these days.

Haven't heard anything about the Paris Hilton Pledge to always wear underwear while getting out of cars. Or the Foot-Long Corn Dog Pledge: never to allow photographers within 30 feet while eating at the State Fair. And let's not forget the Charlie Sheen Career Management Pledge, in which people take an intractable oath not to embarrass everyone they've ever met. Then again, these *are* known politicians.

The Marriage Vow is the one that said black children born into slavery were more likely to be raised by a two-parent family than African-American children today, which some people pointed out almost, kind of, nearly, really close to, endorsed slavery. Little bit. Michele Bachmann admitted signing it, but later recanted, claiming not to have read it.

There you go. Didn't read it. You know what we need? I'll *tell* you what we need. We need candidates to sign a pledge not to sign any pledges they haven't read. And bearing in mind the state of illiteracy currently in evidence, that in itself should cut down on this widespread pledging, considerably.

**Highly Instructive ELECT TO LAUGH! Quote:** "Sensible and responsible women do not want to vote. The relative positions to be assumed by man and woman in the working out of our civilization were assigned long ago by a higher intelligence than ours." Grover Cleveland.

# Prom Queen Anguish

*Just like the rest of us, Republican voters only want what they can't have.*

It's human nature. We want what we can't have. Grass is greener. The romantic lure of the unattainable. Knowledge that high school girls have long since weaponized. Nothing entices a hormonally imbalanced freshman like flouncing down a crowded hall laughing through a gaggle of friends with a flip of the pony-tail and nary a backwards glance. Of course, a short skirt doesn't hurt.

Same holds true in politics. A short skirt doesn't hurt. No matter how many dance partners the Republicans convince to attend their courtship gala, you'd swear their head was on ball bearings the way they keep swiveling to the door to see who might be lurking outside. Waiting for the bad boy rock stars to finish their smokes in the parking lot and make a grand entrance. Or spin out to the highway spitting a rooster-tail of gravel.

Can't blame them. The Right is just getting over its relationship with an older man, which ended badly, and they're hungering for some excitement. The reason they can't get it up for the geeks and dorks and stalwarts like Huntsman and Paul and Santorum and Cain. Oh sure, they're tolerated and marginally encouraged but with an enthusiasm one normally associates with favorite dish-towels and serviceable oil filters. The AV crew. Library boys. Not the smooching kind.

But to the GOP's dismay, all the heartthrobs have left the building. Donald Trump flirted extensively this spring, but then ran away with his true love, reality television, that tramp. Ms. Popular Transfer Student, Sarah Palin, dragged out her coquettish tease so long, even the most bewitched of beaus lost interest. On the rebound, blushing and gushing, Michele Bachmann accepted a corsage, but shortly after was discovered cheating with a corn dog, and jittery suitors fell out of love faster than a middle school girl after Justin Beiber cut his hair.

After extended entreaties, Rick Perry triumphantly waltzed in to the fanfare of a conquering quarterback, and was immediately voted Homecoming King. No more calls, we have a winner. For about a week. Then, the Texas Governor unraveled like a badly knit letter sweater caught in a threshing machine. A series of threshing machines. Seven to ten.

Even he admits he may have stumbled in debate class. Yeah. Stumbled being a polite way of saying "dug a hole deep enough to hide at least half of those very threshers of which earlier we spoke." The more the cheerleaders saw of Captain Haircut, the more the bloom vamoosed the rose. 60 to zero in 5.6.

With the dance but a couple months away, conservatives are frantically whining and pining for a savior to rise from these streets, turning their attention east to woo another Governor, Chris Christie of New Jersey. They're Crazy for Christie. The right Mr. Right. Too big to fail. Flattered, Christie toned down his persistent "Not interested" to a titillating "let's wait and see." Oooh. Shivers.

Christie clearly relishes the role of vamping vixen, but continues to dither, aware that his date is a bit fickle, having discarded prospective partners like Kleenex in the midst of a bad cold. Meanwhile, Mitt Romney patiently waits dressed in his gown standing at the door. Wondering when the GOP will settle down, come to their senses and get their philandering over with. Might want to change out of those heels, and while you're at it, a short skirt doesn't hurt.

**Highly Instructive ELECT TO LAUGH! Quote:** "Democrats are the party that says government will make you smarter, taller, richer and remove the crabgrass on your lawn. Republicans are the party that say government doesn't work, then they get elected and prove it." PJ O'Rourke.

Become a Hyperink reader. Get a special surprise.

Like the book? Support our author and leave a comment!

# VIII.

# The Incumbency Blues

# Or... his secret service nickname is 'smooth.'

Some experts have praised President Barack Obama for performing brilliantly under adverse circumstances while others blame him for everything gone wrong with the planet over the last 3 years from the substandard maple syrup crop in Vermont to the infestation of grunge into country western to the unusually high levels of mercury in domestic tuna. It's a wash, buddy. One circulating discouraging word has it that our Chief Executive is a bit arrogant, but you know what, at least he's smart. Because we tried arrogant and not-so-smart for eight long years and that didn't work. Even his fiercest critics would have to admit the President Obama has undergone some unusual trials. In his first year he was forced to stare down some Somali pirates. Hah. Knew I'd get it in here. Oh sure, Hillary Clinton tried talking tough "Thems that dies is the lucky ones." But the only thing a pirate really fears is a bigger badder pirate. So what we do is convince Obama to stop shaving. Then have his staff constantly refer to him as Blackbeard. Even if the whiskers come in gray, it still works on a couple of levels. Could buy the Secretary of State a bird to perch on her shoulder. And encourage Joe Biden to appear in public wearing an eye patch. Or better yet, a mouth patch. Perhaps send Obama to Pirate School. "Buckle your swash in six easy lessons." Where's our buccaneers? "Sir. Under our buckin' hats, sir!"  And that ain't the half of it as you will see after continued perusal.

# The Honeymoon Is Over

*Investigating the very real possibility of a President being served with divorce papers before returning his rental tux.*

Hey guys, Will Durst here to freak out at what might have been the shortest honeymoon this side of a drunken Britney Spears careening off of quarter poker video games in Vegas. I'm talking about Barack Obama's relationship with the press after his Inauguration as 44th President of the United States. The hands-off grace period might even have edged into negative territory. There was no celebratory carrying over the threshold here. This was more like a sack of potatoes being dropped on the porch. Major veranda dumpage. Honeymoonus interruptus. The epitome of a honeymo.

First he was criticized for giving a workmanlike speech. "Very un-transcendent." "Where's the poetry?" Then, even though he mentioned no names, he was faulted for dissing George W. Bush by declaring that America is ready to lead again, implying that someone, who shall remain nameless, wasn't very lively in that whole "leading" line of activity.

Why stop there? He could also be accused of fostering a frigid climate, failing to float ethereally out to the podium, neglecting to turn the Reflecting Pool into wine, a marked inability to part the Potomac, and not raising Lincoln from the dead. And while we're at it, how come he didn't he use his ears as wind baffles to protect us in the crowd from the briskness?

But that's the media. And that's their job. The rest of America couldn't care less. Wedged tighter than jarred anchovies in the middle of 2 million of their closest friends, the multitudes were just happy to see or hear or even be in the distant vicinity of this defining moment of democracy. For many, it was like going to heaven and coming home. Only they had to walk. Both ways. The Metro lines were so long you'd think it was

Hundred-Dollar Bills Pinned to the Seats Day. And available cabs were like mortgages in South Florida: a charming but totally illusory concept.

Even with all those people, not a single arrest was made. Not that there wasn't any crime. After all, Congress was still in session. But, except for the overriding fear someone might be speared by Aretha Franklin's hat, the day of executive transition was peaceful. The only glitch was when Barack Obama and Supreme Court Head Justice John Roberts danced around the oath like two frozen footed teenagers on a first date. And two Senators went down during the Congressional Lunch. But Ted Kennedy is fine after suffering from fatigue. And 91 year old Robert Byrd quickly recovered from being informed that the new president is a Negro. "What? Fathered two black children? Unnnnnh." Thud!

Dick Cheney garnered much attention in his Dr. Strangelove garb. The enchantment spell must have worn off an hour early. It was reported that the outgoing Vice President was in a wheelchair due to a pulled hamstring while moving boxes. Apparently, even though empty, Pandora needed them back. The Vice-President moving his own boxes. Yeah. I buy that. Or maybe he realized it was the last day of his government job and was trying to weasel some workman's comp.

Finally, to show their affection, the crowd lovingly serenaded George Bush's departing helicopter as it flew overhead. Poor baby. Hardly anybody paid attention to his farewell address, and absolutely nobody asked for a forwarding address. Then again, with the shape he left this country in, let's just put it this way; he is not getting his security deposit back.

**Highly Instructive ELECT TO LAUGH! Quote:** "In most places in the country, voting is looked upon as a right and a duty, but in Chicago, it's a sport." Dick Gregory

# Obama, Year One: A Report Card

*Channeling Mister Chips to hand out grades for the first year of the first term of the 44th POTUS.*

When asked how he thought his first year as 44th POTUS had proceeded, Barack Obama gave himself a B+. To say other parties have been less enthusiastic is like intimating Tiger Woods is unlikely to receive the National Organization of Women's Husband of the Year Award. Although the Northern Hemisphere Divorce Lawyer Association could probably be coerced into throwing a testimonial or two.

Admittedly, there are three camps in the whole "How has Obama Done So Far?" debate. The Right, which has been calling for impeachment since around this time last year, Independents who consider every politician the enemy of the people, and the Left which can be seen wearing their disappointment like the dented chain mail of returning Crusaders.

For those of you wishing to celebrate the occasion, may I mention that the traditional first year anniversary gift is paper. And a piece of photographic paper incriminating Republican Senator, Mitch McConnell, in sexual congress with a Kentucky thoroughbred might be appropriate.

Granted, history will hand out the ultimate grade and you'd have to be a fool to judge an entire Presidency based on 12 months, but this particular fool thinks its not only instructional but also a lot of fun to produce a quarter term report card, so here goes.

**English**. B+. Good understanding of vocabulary words, and the ability to use them correctly. Refreshing to have a President who, when he speaks with a foreign leader, the other guy isn't more eloquent in English as a Second Language.

**History**. C+. Apparently wasn't paying attention during Clinton Health Care instructional in 93. Looks like we'll be forced to repeat this class every sixteen years.

**Geography**. A+. Displays exceptional work habits. Visited more countries in first year than any president in history. Most of that necessary to rebuild the bridges torched by a predecessor whose name momentarily escapes us.

**Mathematics**. Incomplete. Seems to be working with a malfunctioning abacus. Further review by Professors Bernanke and Geithner not expected to help much.

**African American Studies**. B+. Seems to have an innate understanding of the subject.

**Semantics**. B+. Is a conscientious worker. No matter what you think of his policies, you have to admire his ability not to get involved in them.

**Business**. C-. Needs to increase speed and comprehension. Tends to allow himself to be bullied by the louder students.

**Physics**. C. Unable to grasp rudimentary concepts like how every action affecting Congress has an equal, opposite, and totally disagreeable reaction.

**Creative Writing**. A-. Exhibits enormous creativity. Sometimes flights of imagination confuses other students.

**Home Economics**. C. Shows initiative; thinks things through for himself. Must come up with more encouraging phrase than "We're losing jobs at a much slower pace."

**Sex Education**. B+. No visible activity at all. Pleasant change for a Democrat. Helpful to have so many negative role models in Congressional ranks for comparison.

**Physical Education**. Exemplary. Photo of him emerging from Hawaiian surf set off beefcake war with Scott Brown.

**Penmanship**. Satisfactory. Leaves very few fingerprints.

**Home Room Conduct**. Cooperative. Polite. Plays well with others. However, ofttimes fails to stand up for himself.

**General Comments**. Continues to grow in independence. Has problems accepting responsibility. Needs to work on leadership qualities.

**Overall Grade**. B-.

**Highly Instructive ELECT TO LAUGH! Note:** In San Jose, California, a city councilman was re-elected even though he was dead. He wasn't even newly dead. Been dead for a month. Voters had plenty of time to weight the options.

# Obama Gets Osama

*The passing of one of history's best hide and seekers.*

Pull the banner out of storage and string it back across the aircraft carrier. Because this time, Mission Really Accomplished. Barack bested bin Laden. Obama got Osama. Or as Fox News reported, "Alien President Murders Terrorist Brother." Though not a big fan of the whole assassination precept, it would take a stupendously bloodless American to decline the pleasure of hammering a couple of nails into this particular coffin.

The most wanted man on the face of the planet. Found. And you had to admire the way it was done; Seal Team Six firing two warning shots into bin Laden's head. One for each tower. The target was unarmed and never had a chance. That's known as synchronicity. Live by the sneak attack, die by the sneak attack.

President George W. Bush, who famously said: "He can run, but he can't hide," was finally proved right.  Although you got to admit, bin Laden did give it a good run: 9 years, 230 days. Think he might have earned Hide and Seek Grand Master Championship status. An award that alas, must be presented posthumously.

Then the burial at sea, which is just a polite way of saying they kicked his carcass overboard. Which you could not do in the San Francisco Bay, or the EPA would be on your butt like THAT. So fast you would drop your truffled foie gras crostini darling.

It's too bad we ditched him so soon. Mucho bucks could have been raised giving ordinary folks a chance to pose with the corpse like they did back in the Old West. "Get your picture taken with the Mad Architect of Ground Zero. 10 bucks." Could have carted the remains around to County Fairs and Tractor Pulls in a refrigerated casket shoved onto the bed of a Ford F-250. Like what happened with the World Series trophy only with more punching. Eventually the cadaver would find its way to Vegas with its own Cirque du Soleil show, or as one of the stiffer entrants on "Dancing With the Stars."

The Pakistanis aren't happy. But that's redundant. Seriously, have you ever seen a jolly Pakistani? First they claimed to be an integral partner in the operation. Unh-hunh. "Hey old partner, thanks for all the assistance. Here's a broom. Got to go."

Now they're whining we made them look bad. You know, we can't take all the credit for that. Head Honcho Al Qaeda himself living behind your version of West Point and nobody notices? Right. Like Lady Gaga hiding out at the Vatican for six years. One of the blind 80 year-old Cardinals would have sniffed her out. "Blaspheme!"

Bin Laden's safe house reportedly had no phone or internet and burned its trash inside the compound. So, if you think of it, he pretty much was already living in hell. All we did was change the location.

The Seal Team also managed to retrieve a sizable cache of computer disks, which eventually may reveal a vast network of terrorist contacts and sleeper cell structures, but we do know the Saudi Schizo collected porn, used herbal Viagra, and if you believe the videos, hogged the remote. Hate Americans? Hell, looks like he was practicing to be one. Surprised he wasn't wearing a backwards baseball cap. Red Sox. Because he hates the Yanks.

But now, thank god, this whole thing is over and our troops can come home and we won't have to take off our shoes at the airport anymore and can turn our attention to hunting down the next biggest threat to democracy. Of course, we're talking about Wisconsin Governor Scott Walker.

**Highly Instructive ELECT TO LAUGH! Quote:** "In my lifetime, we've gone from Eisenhower to George W Bush. From JFK to Al Gore. If this is evolution, I believe in 20 years, we'll be voting for plants." Lewis Black. (Circa 2000. 8 years to go)

# Watching Sausages

*They fan the flames of stupidity then blame others for the escalating costs of air conditioning.*

Otto Van Bismarck said, "Laws are like sausages, it is better not to see them being made." Sausages? We would have loved to have seen some sausages during the passage of the Patient Protection & Affordable Care Act. We would have killed for sausages. As any Wisconsin boy can tell you, Sheboygan bratwursts cooked over coals until crispy blistered then nestled in butter-grilled buns on top of fried onions slathered with Stadium Sauce can be pretty darn yummy.

What we got was cut-rate, irate hot dogs. The ugly spectacle of Congressional wieners pummeling each other over health care was as appetizing as mixing snail guts and lizard tripe and cephalopod eyeballs with cottage cheese and yellow food dye then serving it on a fungus covered bark chip. And no, I'm not talking about the spinach dip at The Olive Garden.

This isn't a "pox on both their houses" deal either. Like psychic vultures sensing imminent putrefaction, Republicans amplified their pontificating protestations to a high-pitched squeal; piercing enough to annoy canines all across this great Northern Hemisphere of ours.

In the throes of a pseudo-religious ecstasy, one Texas Republican chummed the waters by calling a Michigan Democrat, "Baby Killer," on the floor of the House, frenzying his posse of nitwit accomplices into hurling the N-word, the F-word, half a dozen bricks, a handful of death threats, several mouths full of red hot spittle, gum wrappers, a jewel encrusted black ceramic bird (the stuff that dreams are made of,) two faxed nooses and possibly a bullet.

The conservative party line claimed their Neanderthals were simply playing catch-up to the health care proponents' lead mitten handling of the issue, and suggested Democrats kill the bill to quell the rising tempers. That's right. Fan the flames of stupidity then blame the other side for the scorching climate (different from global warming.) If Republican gall were congealable, we could dam the Caribbean.

And it's STILL not over. To say the GOP is not taking this defeat lying down is like saying freeze dried mustard clumps make for substandard Q-Tips. Within 10 minutes of the President signing the bill, a deluge of 14 state legislatures ignited challenges to the bill's constitutionality. And you wonder why getting anything done in this country is like trying to shovel sand with a pitchfork.

Republicans vowed to go down swinging and they're probably not talking about hiking the Appalachian Trail with each other's wives. Let's be frank: not a single member of the minority voted for the health care bill. Not one. That's not a political party, that's the Borg. "RESISTANCE IS FUTILE."

The reanimated Halloween pumpkin that is Senator Mitch McConnell remains determined to continue the construction of his cement wall of obstructionism turning "The Party of No," into "The Party of Hell No," veering dangerously close to "The Screw You in the Butt with a Sharp Stick Till Your Eyes Bleed Twice Party!"

People may mock Obama for his Messianic glaze, but you got to relish this resurrection of health care which makes Lazarus risen look like a third grade magic trick. Extreme focus a 30x telescope and you can make out the scuff marks on the bill's knees from where it climbed out of the morgue drawer. Maybe now we should hand the President seven loaves and seven fishes to see how many get fed. Or better yet, seven loaves and seven sausages.

**Highly Instructive ELECT TO LAUGH! Quote:** "The success of Sarah Palin and women like her is good for all women—except, of course, those who will end up paying for their own rape kit and stuff. But for everybody else, it's a win-win. Unless you're a gay woman who wants to marry your partner of 20 years. But for most women, the success of conservative women is good for all of us. Unless you believe in evolution. You know—actually, I take it back. The whole thing's a disaster." Tina Fey.

# The Barack Obama Election Year Decathlon

1. The Individual Medley Multiple Issue-Straddle.

2. The Debt Ceiling Crisis Crunch Clean And Jerk. With an emphasis on the jerks.

3. Global Goodwill High Nuclear Hurdle Tour.

4. Extreme Middle of the Road Straightline Walk-Run.

5. Single Weekend 10 State Promise Them Anything Fundraising Marathon.

6. Last Minute Digging Up a Democrat with a Backbone Desperation Relay.

7. The Incredible Disappearing Successful Solar Energy Photo-Op Sprint.

8. The 800 Pound Gorilla that is the Economy Greco-Roman Wrestle.

9. Biting His Tongue While in the Presence of John Boehner Freestyle.

10. The Joe Biden Advanced Obstacle Course. Now with Landmines!

**Highly Instructive ELECT TO LAUGH! Quote:** "I never vote for anyone. I always vote against." WC Fields.

# Evoluting Fabulously

*The chief executive finally flexes his wings and discovers how to use his powers for good.*

A thousand rainbows of congratulations to Barack Obama for bursting out of his own personal policy closet and fabulously proclaiming he believes "same sex couples should be able to get married." Sir! Welcome to the 3rd year of the 2nd decade of the 21st century, sir! You might also want to check out some of the major strides we've been making in the field of communications. And thank you for not smoking.

The President went on to explain he was slow in his transformation because it had taken a while for his thoughts to go Darwinian. Sadly, he stopped short of endorsing transmutation and neglected to hail Hugh Jackman as the best entertainer on the face of the PLANET!

What we witnessed was no eon-eating, natural selection type evolution; this native political animal spontaneously grew flippers and walked on dry land, prodded only by a nudge from the Biden fossil. Come to think of it, maybe flippers aren't the only body parts BHO grew.

You might even call it a chrysalis, with a caterpillar emerging from its cautious cocoon to sprout wings and fly to a lonely position atop the moral high ground previously inhabited by such disparate denizens as Tammy Baldwin, Barney Frank, and unaccountably, Dick Cheney.

As predictable as a brush-back pitch following a grand slam, Republicans began to howl from 8 different vantages. One right-wing rag claimed he "Buckled" on the issue. Others called him the First Waffler. Might be difficult to hide Mitt Romney's eight thousand waffles behind this big one of Obama's, but they'll run it up the flagpole and give it the old prep school try.

Besides, isn't a waffle when you expediently move to a more popular position to curry votes? Meaning this swing-state polarizer is the exact opposite of a waffle. More of an elffaw. Which is waffle backwards. A polf-pilf. Or a yrrek.

Rush Limbaugh jumped into the fray accusing Obama of waging a "War on Marriage." Everything's a "War" with this guy. Bet he calls breakfast a War on Pancakes. Besides, wringing his hands over homosexuality defiling the sanctity of marriage is a tad disingenuous coming from the guy who hired Elton John to sing at his 4th wedding.

The President's supporters worry he might have offended the black church-going community, one of his inviolate bases. But come on, really? Don't you suspect he could be caught naked in a dumpster with a goat and a Portuguese seamstress and still carry the black church-going community? Two goats? Male seamstress?

Opening a conspiratorial can of mutating worms, it has been suggested someone at the Washington Post leaked the Mitt Romney high school gay pranking story and Obama knew he had to poop or get off the pot. Adding to Romney's image problems: do we really want him tackling Belgium and cutting off its hair because he didn't like the way it looked? "They were asking for it."

Michelle Obama's husband disavowed any desire to legalize gay marriage on a federal level, maintaining it should be a states rights issue. Of course, interracial marriage was illegal in 16 states until a Supreme Court decision in 1967 and some people still consider that an abomination. Guess who's whining about this? Yep. Same social invertebrates.

Fine. Let all gay people move to California. We'll take em. Then just try to get your hair cut in Mississippi. Or take ballet lessons in North Carolina. Or raise money in DC. And that right there might just be… the origin of this species.

**Highly Instructive ELECT TO LAUGH! Quote:** "The art of politics consists of knowing precisely when it is necessary to hit an opponent slightly below the belt." Konrad

Adenauer.

Become a Hyperink reader. Get a special surprise.

Like the book? Support our author and leave a comment!

# IX

# A Challenger Rises From the Mean Streets of Bloomfield Hills

# Or... Thurston P. Howell before the Island.

Though richer than most small Balkan nations, Mitt Romney has an enthusiasm problem. Even amongst Republican party stalwarts, he elicits the kind of fervor a lobster has for clarified butter. It was evident during the primary with his staff working impressively to portray an aura of inevitability. Wow. Inevitability. What's that? Some Borg thing? "Resistance is Futile." Sounds like the fifth and final stage of grief. "Oh, all right. I guess. Why not? Go Mitt." Let's see. Who was the last candidate that flaunted an air of inevitability? Oh, that's right, Hillary Clinton. Who, you got to admit, ended up with a halfway decent job. But the former governor of Massachusetts did survive every other candidate leading the polls at one time. Palin. Trump. Bachmann. Perry. Christie. Cain. Gingrich. Santorum. And the same staff thanked the long campaign for making him a better candidate. But I don't know. All he's done for the last five years is run for President. Not sure his learning curve has any more bendy parts left. He just might be electile dysfunctional. But he is the presumptive nominee. Let's find out more, shall we?

# Tone Deaf, Tin-Eared Borg

There's something about Mitt. And whatever it is, some folks are definitely allergic. Maybe they sense he has the same connection to humanity that a drive shaft has to bouillabaisse. Could be because he's worth more than most small Balkan nations. Might be the Mormon thing or perhaps he just smells odd.

It's almost funny. After crushing Newt Gingrich in Florida, the nomination for the Republican primary race was written off as a done deal with Romney all but handed the crown and the beaucoup bouquets reserved for winners. And by his post election strut, you could tell the candidate thought along similar lines. Not measuring the drapes or anything, but definitely photo shopping names for inclusion on the bottom line of a bumper sticker.

But the express train to the Tampa printers derailed on the winter plains of the Midwestern states of Colorado, Minnesota and Missouri with Rick Santorum somehow swooping down to sweep all three. Having had to slap up a different wannabee front-runner every week, Romney must feel like he's playing Whack a Mole with a mallet made out of yogurt soaked cat-hair clippings.

Whatever that something about Mitt is, it causes conservatives to contract the dreaded "Itchy I-Don't-Knows," every time they get close to walking down the aisle with the former governor from Massachusetts. It's a rash that erupts only when Willard's name tops the national polls. A serious knee-buckling case of pre-emptive Buyer's Remorse. Of course the clueless plastic smile of an aged Ken doll hasn't acted as a sufficient antidote either.

The tone-deaf android with the egregious tin-ear claimed he was not concerned about "the very poor." As Randy Jackson might say, "A bit pitchy, dawg." The very next day, apparently concerned that his post elitist message wasn't being taken seriously he hugged Donald Trump. Which would be terrific if he were running for Poster Child of the 1%. More like Poster Child of the .0001% of the 1%.

Someone on his staff needs to tell the candidate he already resembles a police sketch artist rendering of a white-collar criminal. A Harvard MBA voted Most Likely to be Perp-Walked up a Courthouse Steps with a Trench Coat Draped over his Handcuffs. Looks more like Gordon Gekko than Michael Douglas ever did. Go on Mitt. Say it. You know you want to. "Greed is good." Feel better now?

The only people who can relate to this guy are country club chaps with a penchant for calling their wives "lovey." He wasn't groomed, he was assembled out of an Ikea box. "One Male Politician; Standard. Bone White."

Romney won Florida by airing 12,000 ads compared to Gingrich's 300, and doing the same to Rick Santorum should be easier than pudding on a stick, since the former Pennsylvania Senator is financing his campaign mostly through bake sales and scrounging under couch cushions.

Santorum actually brags about being so frugal he flies middle seats on United to campaign stops. Seriously? We're supposed to hand the Presidency to a guy who can't find anybody on his staff who can work a seat locater map on an airline website?

Something else about Mitt is he's an absolute blooming chameleon. And over the next couple of weeks, expect to be treated to the Borg Candidate assimilating Santorum's passion for fighting the culture wars with the megaphone turned up to LOUD. Who knows, Mitt could well decide to go all in. And start wearing sweater vests.

**Highly Instructive ELECT TO LAUGH! Quote:** "People don't vote due to ignorance or apathy. And why that is nobody knows and fewer care." Anonymous.

# Shaking the Fleas Off My Dogma

*They don't call him Willard for nothing. Actually they don't call him Willard but you catch my drift.*

Remember way back when his own staffer said Mitt Romney had the convictions of an Etch-A-Sketch? Well, stand back, because as we speak, the former Governor of Massachusetts is being flipped over and shaken so hard the fillings in the back teeth of his whole family are starting to rattle and cascade like some great crumbling Utah Butte.

Fear not the rubble, little ones. This simply means we're entering general election territory, so anything Mitt Romney might have said during the primary... no longer applies. We're beginning anew. Reshuffling the deck. The winter of mass GOP discontent has been made glorious summer by this Son of Dork.

We're not even playing the same ballgame anymore. Fast pitch hardball has morphed into beach volleyball before our very eyes. And the sand's been replaced with money. Unlike the previous six months, the object is no longer about how hard you hit the ball, rather how long it stays in the air. On your side of the net. You may recall this from pre-video game childhood as Keep Away.

A Republican primary is consumed with hard right angles. No quarter asked for, no quarter given. The general election is much more soft focus. Nice round spongy contours. Less muscular retorts, more sly evasions. Gauze is being spread over the lens and next comes the two fingers of Vaseline. Best keep a towel handy.

Already the severely conservative former governor has turned into a moderate kind of a regular guy. Mr. Hyde sunk behind the lab island and Doctor Jeckyl rose to walk forward with an outreached hand. Mister "Its okay to call Susan Fluke a slut" is now the soul of Chivalry.

And the "War on Women" was instigated by Obama. Never mind the hundreds of bills written and enacted across the country by his party restricting rights of women, wholeheartedly endorsed by the candidate. Never mind his previous statements on Planned Parenthood and birth control. Never mind he thinks Lilly Ledbetter is a successfully repressed embarrassing affliction from his youth.

All that silly suffragette bashing has been offset by a single Democrat suggesting Ann Romney might not be qualified to be her husband's economic strategist since she spent her working life running a tycoon's household. Maybe Alice from the Brady Bunch shouldn't be Secretary of the Treasury.

The outcry was so loud a million apple pies shook off of shelves and the President of the United States got tangled in a War on Moms Web. Was this an exceptionally sticky birthday gift to a two-Cadillacked woman or what?

The presumptive nominee is taking a page straight out of the Karl Rove Handbook and plans to run one of those "I know you are, but what am I" campaigns. Later to be partnered with an auspicious "I am rubber, you are glue" ploy.

Republicans love this third grade playground strategy. You indict the other guy for exactly what you're guilty of. Go back to 2004, when a borderline deserter successfully accused a war hero of being a traitor. The theory being: if you can't convince the people, confuse them. As the right is so fond of preaching: there's such a fine line between educated and confused.

It's only a matter of time before Romney accuses Obama of being a flip-flopper extraordinaire. A fat cat tool of Wall Street. Totally out of touch with normal people. Trying to gut Social Security. Belongs to a funny religion. With a long history of extreme insensitivity to dogs. And he has cooties.

**Highly Instructive ELECT TO LAUGH! Quote:** "Vote: the instrument and symbol of a free man's power to make a fool of himself and a wreck of his country." Ambrose Bierce.

# Romney Inc.

*Diving into the Super PAC pool without benefit of water wings but self-inflating my trunks.*

No. It's not over. Well, okay, it's kind of over. But the Republican nomination is not totally-otally over. As it very well should be. How over? So over, the fat lady has not only sung, she's back in her hotel room kicking off her shoes easing into a recliner with the remote in one hand and digging deep into a two pound box of marzipan with the other. Yes, that over.

Could have nailed this puppy to the headboard a month ago, but after every sledgehammer-type primary door slam, Team Romney somehow manages to stumble in bright media glare on dead flat asphalt, ripping knees out of focus group-approved perfectly faded jeans, to lay bleeding on the tarmac.

First it was "likes to be able to fire people," then "not concerned about the very poor." But now all those allusions to the front runner being a distant android or impassive cyborg or corporatized zombie have been shelved because one of his own staffers offered up a more perfect crystallization: the Etch-A-Sketch candidate. The major difference being, the child's toy works via magnetism, a concept that continues to elude the former Governor of Massachusetts.

Hard to imagine a worse, more apt toy analogy. Gumby, perhaps. Yo-Yo Man. Slip and Slide. Speak and Spell. Silly String. The Slinky. Chutes and Ladders. Mister Potato Head. No, wait. That's Newt. Funny thing is, Bain Capital owns Toys R Us, so Mitt will make money off his opponents' frenzied press conference accessorizings. Never let anything including embarrassment get in the way of profit, eh Mitt? Truly, you are a malleably nimble free marketeer.

Due to his chronic electile dysfunctionalism, Romney must accept responsibility for imbuing this race with its semblance of contest. In Fits and Spurts, and other proud Southern states. Every time a new contender pops up, however, the Super PAC country club types at Romney Inc. immediately conspire to pummel Candidate X with such a tsunami of negative ads that before long, Candidate X's own family harbors misgivings about lunching with the kids. "Don't forget. If uncle touches you in a bad place, use the whistle."

Outspent 17 to 1 in Florida, Newt Gingrich provided the initial target of a patented Romney Inc. Airwave Carpet-Bombing™. Now, fast forward, first to Michigan, and again to Illinois, with the victim named Rick Santorum; who continues to ooze from self-inflicted palm wounds, vainly praying that devout outrage can surmount pockets deeper than the Mariana Trench.

Mitt hasn't lost this nomination. Yet. But neither is he winning. His Super PAC is buying it for him like a dented TV console at an Everything For A Dollar Store year-end sale. This is all about money. Recent election results and pure motivation of his cadre of corporate cronies. Romney Inc. realizes fortunes can be exponentially multiplied if the government gets out of the taxation and regulation business. So, that's the plan, man.

And, as we all know, it takes money to make money. Money talks and other stuff walks. Money makes the world go round, and while money can't buy you happiness, it looks more and more like it can buy Romney Inc. top slot on the 2012 Republican presidential ticket. And once that happens, the Etch-A-Sketch will be turned over and severely shaken with its dizzy base profoundly unstirred.

**Highly Instructive ELECT TO LAUGH! Quote:** "If you don't vote, you can't bitch. Then again, I'll pick up the slack for both of us." Will Durst.

# Not-So-Rabid GOP Endorsements for Mitt Romney

"Not the brainwashed Romney. That was his dad."

"Only 2 of his sons think he's a soulless Cyborg."

"Not the kind of guy who would hold you down and cut your hair, unless you were really asking for it."

"Pretty down to earth for someone building a 57 room beachfront mansion in La Jolla with a car elevator."

"Survived the mean streets of Bloomfield Hills."

"A man who stands by his previous statements, no matter what they are."

"He's no Newt Gingrich."

"Determined to make the world safe for rich people."

"He's Oxymormonic!"

"Hasn't strapped a dog to the roof of his car in over 28 years."

"Mitt Romney. He's got gas money."

"Never ridden a bus in his entire life."

"Such an outsider, doesn't even know where DC is."

"Mitt Romney. A man who feels strongly about both sides of many issues."

**Highly Instructive ELECT TO LAUGH! Quote:** "I offer my opponents a bargain. If they stop telling lies about us, I will stop telling the truth about them." Adlai Stevenson.

# The Potemkin Candidate

*Speaking to the spectacle of the shape-shifter candidate emeritus.*

Permanently capitalizing the P in Presumptive Nominee, the Texas primary shoved Mitt Romney right over the delegate precipice, and now with the nomination dangling from the third finger of his left hand, the campaign has taken a sudden turn towards the nebulous. Ambiguous Ville. The theory being, candidates shouldn't make mistakes in the murky bog of summer. Even when they do, the atmosphere is too hazy to notice.

One advantage to this smoky amorphous strategy is it plays directly to the man's strengths. The former governor of Massachusetts doesn't have what you might call an actual personality. He's more of a virgin canvas. A good-looking blank slate onto which any number of convictions and philosophies can be believably projected. He's the coloring-book and we voters the crayons. And no fighting over who gets to be burnt sienna.

One of the major pitfalls inherent to this kind of approach is the strong jawed father of five strapping boys just might play the part too well and come to epitomize what Gertrude Stein said about Oakland: "There's no there there." Makes a void look cluttered.

Nobody in the GOP wants to be associated in any way with Oakland, much less have the top of the ticket become a patron saint. The Potemkin Candidate needs to project a quality more substantial than some shape shifter with a supernatural ability to assume the identity of whoever or whatever they plant next to him. Probably why you don't see many Romney rallies held at zoos. Too afraid he'll pass by a chameleon cage and turn green.

Another potential mine in the Road to Tampa is the struggle to keep Willard from hanging out with the wrong crowd. You know, other Republicans. Especially distressing to see him palling around with Donald Trump. Again. Like being photographed at a clown convention. No matter how hard you try, some of that white face is bound to wipe off on even the most ghostly of political shadows.

Donald Trump: a man who is to sober judgment what chocolate sprinkles are to quantum physics. Fueling more fickle-furnaces that suspect he'll say or do anything to get to

50.1%, Romney refuses to criticize The Donald, even when the reality show host spouts further Birther nonsense. "Obama was born in Kenya." No, he wasn't. He was born in Honolulu. In a manger. Everybody knows that.

When asked why he continues to press on with this discredited charge, Trump said: "People on the street tell me not to give up on the issue." Donald, for crum's sake, you live in New York City. People on the street also say "My underwear sprouted wings and is made out of plutonium."

Although when you think about it, the Oxymormon needs to pick a vice president who makes him look presidential, and The Donald certainly does that. He also makes Lou Ferrigno look Presidential. Bernie Madoff. Some random guy in a banana suit twirling a sign.

Of course, featuring these two titans of industry, people would either flock to or flee from the Vulture Capitalist Ticket. You've heard of Dumb & Dumber? Welcome to Rich & Richer. Even George Will would have to admit, it's a paring that would go a long way into nailing down the bloviating ignoramus vote. Start cranking out the bumper stickers: "Romney/ Trump 2012. We Like to Fire People!"

**Highly Instructive ELECT TO LAUGH! Note:** In 1920, one vote was the difference in the state of Tennessee's decision to ratify the 19th amendment giving women the right to vote. Tennessee was the deciding state making the amendment law.

# The Bain of His Electoral Existence

*The corporate trader who traded Massachusetts board member to Utah for a luger to be named later.*

You might say it was a turbulent week for Mitt Romney. You could also say a light lemon sugar wash makes for ineffective mosquito repellent. He claims to have totally left Bain Capital to run the 2002 Salt Lake City Winter Olympics even though his company handed the government multiple signed documents stating otherwise and now financial questions plague his campaign like a swarm of dive-bombing bees in a bathroom stall.

The presumptive GOP nominee finds himself in the uncomfortable position of having to convince skeptical voters someone can serve as a firm's CEO, President, Chairman of the Board, sole stockholder, junior janitor, cafeteria server in a plastic hairnet, and still have absolutely nothing to do with the direction of the company. And who's going to believe that? Except anybody who has ever worked in a major corporation.

It boils down to whether he played any active role after leaving in 1999 and his subsequent retroactive retirement. Whatever that means. He says no, and all those SEC filings listing him as boss were simply corporate publicity moves like Donald Trump putting his name on various hotels and statuesque fashion models. Which many psychologists define as an edifice complex.

Adding to the confusion, in 2002, Willard successfully disputed tax records listing him as an inhabitant of Utah because he was required to have 7 year residency in Massachusetts for gubernatorial eligibility. Then again, who would quarrel with having a president who could be in two places at the same time.

During the period in question, Romney does admit to sitting on the board of a corporation called LifeLike, which co-incidentally seems to be his campaign slogan. Seriously? Board member, or beta-test prototype? But after some investigation, we're pretty sure they had nothing to do with his construction. Turns out, they make dolls, not puppets.

The reason this is all so important is because Romney declares his qualifications stem from his recognized business acumen. And if it's proven he either lied under oath or to the American people, it would go a long way into establishing he truly does deserve national office.

Romney maintains he is totally within the law not releasing any more tax records than required. Yeah, well, in certain states gambling and prostitution and foie gras are within the law as well. Is this guy running for the presidency or trying to avoid the constabulary?

The former Governor from Massachusetts rationalizes he's only following in Teresa Heinz's 04 footsteps. But Teresa Heinz wasn't running for President. Her husband, John Kerry was, and he released 20 years of taxes. So, maybe Romney is subliminally letting us know the post he's really angling for is… First Lady.

Speaking of which, presumptuous presumptive Marie Antoinette understudy, Ann Romney, addressed the subject with "we've given all you people need to know." Wow. Now, we're "you people." Might be taking that Mormon Royalty thing a bit too far. Fortunately, her husband was able to refrain from using that term addressing the NAACP.

Come on Mitt. In the biggest of all poker games, you're at the final table and it's time to go all in. Like the police always tell us when they start ramping up surveillance, "The innocent have nothing to fear." You're squeaky clean, right? Or is this just another example of that age old Golden Rule: "He who has the gold, makes the rules."

**Highly Instructive ELECT TO LAUGH! Note:** Henry Clay (1824, 1832, & 1844) & William Jennings Bryan (1896, 1900, 1908) each lost 3 Presidential elections. The Buffalo Bills appeared in 4 consecutive Super Bowls, (1991-1994) and lost them all. Will Durst was a Phone-A-Friend on "Who Wants to Be a Millionaire" and cost his buddy Rudy Reber a quarter of a million dollars.

# Possible Skeletons Buried in the Mitt Romney Tax Crypts

- Not just a bank account in the Cayman Islands; owns two of the Cayman Islands.

- Tithes 10% of income every year to… Scientology.

- Claims 9 kids as dependents.

- Collects royalties from Kraft Foods for trademarked product "Preppy Dip."

- Turns out Mitt really IS short for Mittens.

- In 2004, he wrote off $60,000 in Chinese made hair products.

- Holds 60% of Greece's debt.

- Back in the late 80s, his closest business associate was Pablo Escobar.

- Top three charitable donations: Greenpeace, Planned Parenthood & Code Pink.

- Swiss bank account number is 666.

- Served 18 months in prison for tax evasion while governor of Massachusetts and nobody noticed. Known in the yard as Shifty.

- Holds lease on a 120,000 square foot warehouse in Nevada filled with sex toys.

- Yearly health care deductions include three pages for nickel-metal-hydride batteries.

- Entire estate has been placed under the control of Rafalca, the Olympic horse.

- Claims Newt Gingrich books-on-tape as therapeutic deductions.

- The state of South Dakota is in his IRA.

- Not only paid no taxes 1990-2002, turns out we owe him $400,000,000.

**Highly Instructive ELECT TO LAUGH! Quote:** "Those who are too smart to engage in politics are punished by being governed by those who are dumber." Plato.

# A Staggeringly Stumbling Trip

*Very few of the guide books include helpful suggestions for itineraries such as this.*

Mitt Romney has to be more relieved than an Iowa corn farmer in the middle of a thunderstorm to be back on home soil. Arms wide. Head back. Wet face. Smile. Podium steps. National Anthem.

The American electorate may harbor an ambivalent attitude towards the former governor of Massachusetts, but the reaction to his European Vacation from folks across the big pond could only be described as decisively derisive. If diplomacy were a hurdling sport, the guy stumbled over the lane chalk.

The plan was for the GOP nominee to embark on a low-risk, three-country jaunt to raise suspect foreign policy bona fides, but the six-day charm offensive proved to be light on charm and heavy on the offense. Good will hunting transformed into ill will gathering.

The first stop was Great Britain, where the Wee Bairne of Bain managed to pretty much insult the whole country. Romney told an interviewer that security problems surrounding the Olympics were disconcerting. And the gates of Hades opened and all sorts of evil tabloid creatures sprung forth.

He only said the same exact thing they themselves had been saying for weeks in Merry Olde, but you know family. Siblings are allowed to call their father a harebrained lovable loser: cousins, not so much.

David Cameron snapped London was a busy, world-class city, and "not in the middle of nowhere" which some interpreted as a snub targeting the man who famously saved the 2002 Winter Olympics. But the Prime Minister only demonstrated his own geographic ineptitude. Salt Lake City isn't in the middle of nowhere; it's in Utah.

Ann Romney traipsed along to offer moral support to her horse Rafalca, competing in Olympic dressage. Dressage being a French event where horse and rider perform predetermined movements. Like inter-species dancing. Which you'd think would be illegal in Utah.

The Overseas Gaffe Express then moved to the Middle East where Mr. Romney stuck a prayer in the Wailing Wall, presumably pleading to be struck dumb. Retroactively. Later he gave a speech saying Israel's financial acumen and culture provided it with a major advantage over Palestine. Which sort of ticked off the Palestinians. Not to mention a couple of Israelis who thought he called them thrifty.

The trip landed for a final stop in Poland and everyone held their breath. But all that happened on the outskirts of the evil continent of Europe was an aide cautioned a reporter to stop peppering the candidate with questions because they were in a holy site for Poles. And to emphasize the sanctity of the joint, he entreated the reporter to kiss his butt. Only he didn't say butt, rather the word that rhymes with class. A quality of which the aide is obviously bereft.

The campaign was hoping to use this journey abroad to muffle the outcry over tax returns and set up the Vice Presidential pick, but now even the most partisan Republican has to wonder how many consecutive blows to the head their candidate can take without visible bruising. Need to line up a platoon of make up artists for Tampa.

Britain, Israel, and Poland. Not what you call the Group of Death. Those aren't the tough ones, Mitt. Got to rate their collective degree of difficulty in diplomatic terms at about a negative 2. But one thing you got to give him—he stuck his dismount.

**Highly Instructive ELECT TO LAUGH! Note:** Only two Presidents to run unopposed were George Washington, (both terms) and James Monroe. (2nd term) Also the only two presidents with national capitals named after them. Washington D.C. & Monrovia, Liberia.

Become a Hyperink reader. Get a special surprise.

Like the book? Support our author and leave a comment!

# X.

# The Most Important Election in the History of America. Again.

# Or... one of these guys is going to win? Seriously?

From out of the green mist enveloping the campaign doldrums they come. Relentlessly. Doggedly. Cattedly. Trudging blank-faced and soulless. Armies of cash hungry zombies brandishing partisan pickaxes, shovels and crowbars, with only one goal rattling around their feverish brains. Campaign booty. Pieces of 8. Entire 8s. Eight figured 8s. Negative ads don't grow on trees you know. The peripatetic participants are as frenzied as reef sharks in shallow tuna-rich waters trying to raise a little bit of money here, some more money there, how about all that money everywhere. Staffs are so laser-focused you'd think they were pursued by the hounds of fund-raising hell. Maybe they are. Or the ghost of John McCain's 08 late October. Don't bother asking what the big time donors get for their greenbacks; you don't want to know. That's the dark side of Democracy: those that give, get. Face it: in America today, the major difference between a campaign contribution and a bribe is five syllables. The cynical among us might say we no longer bother engaging in elections, we conduct auctions. But like everything else in this country, at least they're big. And loud. And expensive. And this one is dead ahead.

# The Mitt Romney/ Barack Obama Face Off

| | Mitt Romney | Barack Obama |
|---|---|---|
| Music Television | American Bandstand | MTV Raps |
| Talk Show Host | Leno | Letterman |
| Gilligan's Island | Thurston P. Howell III | The Professor |
| Mary Anne/ Ginger | Lovie | Both |
| News | Bill O'Reilly | PBS News Hour |
| Sitcom | Leave it to Beaver | Modern Family |
| Movie | Wall Street | Blues Brothers |
| Musical | Book of Mormon | In The Heights |
| Road Food | Big Mac | Five Guys Double no bun |
| Soft Drink | Caffeine Free Diet Coke | Dr. Pepper |
| Blues Artist | Randy Travis | Robert Cray |
| Comedian | Ray Romano | Chris Rock |
| Jeans | Wrangler No Wrinkle | Levis Mom Jeans |
| Cop show | Dragnet | Life on Mars (BBC) |
| Sports Show | Sportscenter | NCAA Bracket Busters |
| President | Ronald Reagan | Abraham Lincoln |
| Newspaper | Wall Street Journal | Chicago Reader |
| Magazine | Fortune | Scientific American |
| Bloviator | Rush Limbaugh | Rachel Maddow |
| Car | Lincoln Navigator | Lincoln Navigator |

| | | |
|---|---|---|
| **Necessary Albatross** | Newt Gingrich | Joe Biden |
| **Uninvited Albatross** | Ted Nugent | Hilary Rosen |
| **Superhero** | Superman | Northstar |
| **Athlete** | Roger Maris | Dwayne Wade |
| **Oldies** | Beach Boys | Ernie K. Doe |
| **James Bond** | George Lazenby | Daniel Craig |
| **US Landmark** | Mount Rushmore | Road to Hana |
| **Arch Enemy** | Michael Moore | Dick Cheney |
| **Sport** | Equestrian Dressage | H-O-R-S-E |
| **Historical Document** | Diary of Joseph Smith Jr. | Emancipation Proclamation |
| **Warrior Princess** | Wonder Woman | Michelle Obama |
| **Comfort Food** | Meatloaf | Italian Beef Sandwich |
| **Guilty Pleasure** | Gossip Girl | NCIS |
| **Cocktail** | Shirley Temple | Martini, shaken not stirred |
| **Author** | Danielle Steele | Ovid |
| **iPod Fave** | "Cherish." | "Ball of Confusion." |

**Highly Instructive ELECT TO LAUGH! Quote:** "Politics is the gentle art of getting votes from the poor and campaign funds from the rich by promising to protect each from the other." Oscar Ameringer.

# Romney or Manson

*A short instructive quiz.*

Who's responsible for the quotes here? Charles Milles Manson or Willard Mitt Romney?

1. I made a difference. I put in place the things I wanted to do.

2. Never thought I was normal. Never tried to be normal.

3. You sit down with your attorneys, and they tell you what you have to do.

4. I purchased a gun when I was a young man.

5. There's no plates like chrome for the hollandaise.

6. It's worse than a fairy tale.

7. We used to have some cosmic gatherings back in the mountains that would probably shake a Mormon Tabernacle Choir's eardrums.

8. Good for some may not be the same for others.

9. Everybody is on my list. I'm not taking anybody off my list, alright?

10. I told them that anything they do for their brothers and sisters is good if they do it with a good thought.

11. The train's hard. The road's rough.

12. Corporations are people, my friend.

13. I should tell my story. I'm also unemployed.

14. I like to fire people who provide me services.

15. If you are going to do something, do it well.

16. Getting up every day and going through this again and again is hard.

17. I tasted a beer and tried a cigarette as a wayward teenager and never did it again.

18. I like those fancy raincoats you bought. Really sprung for the big bucks.

19. I know and understand you are much more than what I think you are but first I must deal with you the way I think of you even if that's only my thinking and not you.

20. I'm not familiar precisely with exactly what I said, but I stand by what I said, no matter what it was.

**Answers:**

- 1. 2. 6. 7. 8. 10. 11. 15. 16. 19. Charles Manson

- 3. 4. 5. 9.  12. 13. 14. 17. 18. 20. Mitt Romney

**Highly Instructive ELECT TO LAUGH! Quote:** "Majority rule only works if you consider individual rights. You can't have 5 wolves and 1 sheep voting on what to have for dinner." Benjamin Franklin.

# The Bold Choice

*Positive proof that the appeal of Paul Ryan lies on both sides of the aisle.*

With the election slipping away like a handful of mercury on a turbocharged Merry-Go-Round, Mitt Romney managed to change the conversation from unreleased tax returns and foreign misadventures by plucking Paul Ryan out of the Wisconsin wilds to be his running mate. "Romney-Ryan." Short, alliterative and one syllable more conservative than "Obama-Biden."

The situation appeared so desperate, the choice couldn't wait until after Closing Ceremonies of the Olympics, forcing the House Budget Committee Chairman to share the weekend spotlight with enough English pop stars to clear out the hairspray aisle at 7 Boots' drug stores. The Republican Congressman may be famous for his P90x work-out regimen, but the Spice Girls have much better legs. And they're way older.

Ryan was universally hailed as a bold choice. Yeah, well, maybe, but bold is not necessarily synonymous with good. Whiskey for breakfast is a bold choice. Spun glass underwear is bold. Forehead dragon tattoos. Passing an 18 wheeler on a blind curve doing 80 in the rain. Incredibly bold. Not necessarily smart.

Another white male Christian conservative. That is bold. But only when NOT compared to absolutely anything else. It's been speculated a major reason for awarding the Wisconsin Congressman prize spot at the bottom of the bumper sticker was to energize the base. And total slam-dunk there. The question is: which base?

Republicans are shaking like a Brazilian supermodel on a Lake Superior beach shoot in January. Only, happier. Haven't seen them this excited since John McCain hooked up with some governor of Alaska. Meanwhile, Democrats are salivating so uncontrollably, they'd be advised to invest in bibs to keep from soiling their 5 thousand dollar Man-of-the-People suits.

A coordinated attack was immediately launched to trash Ryan's Path to Prosperity budget bill, which replaces Medicare with vouchers. But the Romney campaign instantly counter-accused the President of gutting Medicare to the tune of $700 billion for ObamaCare. So we got that to look forward to: 11 more weeks of the echoing refrain of

"You're killing Medicare," "No, you're killing Medicare." Rinse and repeat. And repeat again. Continue rinsing.

Ryan, a self-professed Ayn Rand acolyte, was forced to denounce his Objectivism hero when somebody on his staff who reads discovered Ms. Rand rejected all forms of religion, which some might infer meant she did not believe in Jesus. You can love one or the other, but not both. Like with Wham!

Allegations also arose that while Ryan ladled scorn onto the stimulus bill, he wrote 4 letters to the Secretary of Energy praising programs and requesting funds for his district. Could this be a fount of flip for Mitt's famed flop?

Ryan blamed Obama for a GM plant closing in Janesville in December of 2008. When George Bush was still president. And the Titanic: that was Obama too. The Hindenburg, no, that was Biden.

The wealthy son of a Janesville, Wisconsin highway contractor doesn't do much to help with Romney's Richie Rich problem either. In March, he was forced to amend his financial disclosure statement, having forgotten to include a $5 million trust account. Then again, who among us hasn't forgotten a multi million dollar trust account? "Now where did I put that pesky Five Mil? Must be in my other pants pockets."

Difficult to discern whether the GOP Boy Wonder is helping or hindering Willard's ticket. But if the campaign arc doesn't start levitating real soon, he might be forced to release some tax returns just to change the conversation. Again.

**Highly Instructive ELECT TO LAUGH! Note:** In the 1824 Presidential election, Andrew Jackson won the most popular votes and the most electoral votes (99) but not a plurality so the contest was sent to the House, which gave the election to John Quincy Adams. (84) The other two aspirants were William Crawford (43) and Henry Clay. (37) All four ran on the Democratic-Republican ticket.

# The Many Moods of Mitt Romney

| Winsome | Querulous | Resolute |
| Scrappy | Fretful | Vivacious |
| Bubbly | Volatile | Whimsical |

**Highly Instructive ELECT TO LAUGH! Quote:** "Anybody who can be elected—pretty much shouldn't be." Will Durst.

# Who Will Win & Why

*The crux of the matter.*

- Romney will win because his name isn't Hussein.

- Obama will win because his name isn't Willard.

- Romney will win because he's never been photographed riding a mountain bike.

- Obama will win because he's never been photographed sitting behind his wife on a jet ski.

- Romney will win because he knows business.

- Obama will win because he knows people.

- Romney will win because he knows the right people.

- Obama will win because he knows the other people.

- Romney will win because of the economy.

- Obama will win because of the economy.

- Romney will win because he has the money.

- Obama will win because he has a soul.

- Romney will win because his Republican compatriots want it more and will do whatever it takes.

- Obama will win because his Democratic compatriots want it enough to quit fighting each other.

- Romney will win because the Republicans are better at fighting dirty.

- Obama will win because America is sick and tired of dirty fighting.

- Romney will win because he makes us feel affluent.

- Obama will win because he makes us feel smart.

- Romney will win because he wasn't born in Kenya.

- Obama will win because he wasn't born in Kenya.

- Romney will win because people with money can count on him.

- Obama will win because people without money count him as one of theirs.

- Romney will win because he's confident.

- Obama will win because he's credible.

- Romney will win because NASCAR Dads don't want to be girlie men.

- Obama will win because Soccer Moms just want their support checks to arrive on time.

- Romney will win because he's prettier.

- Obama wil win because he's taller.

- Romney will win because Ann won't let him lose.

- Obama will win because Michelle will make it happen.

- Romney will win because Obama will run out of money.

- Obama will win because Romney's batteries will drain empty.

- Romney will win because we all want to be rich.

- Obama will win because we all want to be smooth.

- Romney will win because dark forces will gather behind him.

- Obama will win because the Force will be with him. Always.

- Romney will win because his Super PACs will blow Obama out of the water in swing states.

- Obama will win because his Super PACs will pummel Romney as outsourcer-in-chief in swing states.

- Romney will win because his performance in the debates will be disregarded as the result of over-preparation.

- Obama will win because his performance in the debates will be discounted as the consequence of not getting enough sleep.

- Romney will win because he is a latter day Saint.

- Obama will win because of the halo that surrounds him.

- Romney will win because he isn't Obama.

- Obama will win because he isn't Romney.

- Romney will win because of Joe Biden.

- Obama will win because of Paul Ryan.

- Romney will win because he never ate a dog.

- Obama will win because he never strapped a dog to the roof of his car.

- Romney will win because he's not black.

- Obama will win because he's not Mormon.

- Romney will win because of Obama Care.

- Obama will win because of Romney Care.

- Romney will win because he gets more popular votes.

- Obama will win because he gets more electoral votes.

**Highly Instructive ELECT TO LAUGH! Quote:** "Don't forget. Democrats vote on Tuesday, November 6th. Republicans on Wednesday, November 7th." Will Durst.

# Acknowledgements

Need to thank the brave and steadfast Ivory Madison, of Redroom, without whose resolute encouragement and gentle needling none of this would have been possible. And Cari Dawson-Bartley and Robert Bartley at Cagle Cartoons for going so high and above the normal call of duty they probably annoyed NASA by interfering with satellite traffic. And Glenn Schwartz of Cyberlaff for continued faith. Not to forget all the good people at The Marsh for letting me work out my performance anxieties. And last but definitely not least, my lovely wife Debi Ann. Thanks babe. Noon Tuesday.

Become a Hyperink reader. Get a special surprise.

Like the book? Support our author and leave a comment!

# Will Durst

Considered by peers and press as one of the premier political comics in the country, Will Durst has patched together a many-colored quilt of a comedy career. He writes a weekly national political humor column syndicated by Cagle Cartoons, voices commercials and commentaries, yet manages to perform hundreds of gigs a year in theaters and clubs and for corporate events and benefits. His abiding motto is "You can't make stuff up like this." He is a 5-time Emmy nominee; has been fired by PBS three times; told jokes in 14 countries; racked up 7 nominations for Stand-Up of the Year; and his 800+ television appearances include Letterman, HBO, Showtime, CNN, ABC, CBS, NBC, MSNBC, Fox News, the BBC, and many more. The critically acclaimed Off-Broadway run of his one man show: "The All American Sport of Bipartisan Bashing," was turned into his first book. His hobbies include pinball, the never-ending quest for the perfect cheeseburger, and his heroes remain the same as when he was 12... Thomas Jefferson and Bugs Bunny. He lives in the Sunset district of San Francisco with his lovely wife, Debi Ann, and their two cats Eloise and Madaleine, all three of which are, alas, light years funnier than he.

Cover image courtesy of Jeannene Hansen.

Author photo courtesy of Dan Dion.

# About the Publisher

**Hyperink is the easiest way for anyone to publish a beautiful, high-quality book.**

We work closely with subject matter experts to create each book. We cover topics ranging from higher education to job recruiting, from Android apps marketing to barefoot running.

If you have interesting knowledge that people are willing to pay for, especially if you've already produced content on the topic, please reach out to us! There's no writing required and it's a unique opportunity to build your own brand and earn royalties.

Hyperink is based in SF and actively hiring people who want to shape publishing's future. Email us if you'd like to meet our team!

**Note:** If you're reading this book in print or on a device that's not web-enabled, **please email** books@hyperinkpress.com with the title of this book in the subject line. We'll send you a PDF copy, so you can access all of the great content we've included as clickable links.

**Get in touch:**  f

Made in the USA
Charleston, SC
20 December 2012